AIR CAMPAIGN

# AFGHANISTAN 1979–88

Soviet air power against the *mujahideen*

MARK GALEOTTI | ILLUSTRATED BY EDOUARD A. GROULT

OSPREY PUBLISHING
Bloomsbury Publishing Plc
Kemp House, Chawley Park, Cumnor Hill, Oxford OX2 9PH, UK
29 Earlsfort Terrace, Dublin 2, Ireland
1385 Broadway, 5th Floor, New York, NY 10018, USA
E-mail: info@ospreypublishing.com
www.ospreypublishing.com

OSPREY is a trademark of Osprey Publishing Ltd

First published in Great Britain in 2023

A catalogue record for this book is available from the British Library.

ISBN: PB 9781472850713; eBook 9781472850737;
ePDF 9781472850744; XML 9781472850720

23 24 25 26 27  10 9 8 7 6 5 4 3 2 1

Maps by www.bounford.com
Diagrams by Adam Tooby
3D BEVs by Paul Kime
Index by Alan Rutter
Typeset by PDQ Digital Media Solutions, Bungay, UK
Printed and bound in India by Replika Press Private Ltd.

FSC
www.fsc.org
®
MIX
Paper from
responsible sources
FSC® C016779

Osprey Publishing supports the Woodland Trust, the UK's leading woodland conservation
charity.

To find out more about our authors and books visit www.ospreypublishing.com. Here
you will find extracts, author interviews, details of forthcoming events and the option to
sign up for our newsletter.

**Author's note:**
For Cyrillic, I have chosen to transliterate names as they are pronounced, and have
ignored the diacritical 'soft' and 'hard' signs found in the original.
The only exceptions are names that have acquired common forms in English – for
example, 'Gorbachev' rather than the phonetically correct 'Gorbachov'.
Afghanistan has two main languages, *Pashto* and *Dari*, and I have generally stuck to the
most widely used renditions.
Quotations without any reference come from interviews with Soviet veterans carried out
by the author in 1988–91 or later, in post-Soviet Russia or Ukraine.

For an explanation of abbreviations used in the book, please see the Glossary on page 94.

AIR CAMPAIGN

# CONTENTS

# INTRODUCTION

When Soviet tanks rolled into Afghanistan on 27 December 1979, it was intended to be a brief show of force to instal a new and more biddable leader of the People's Democratic Party of Afghanistan (PDPA) and overawe a rural rebellion.[1] After all, under Hafizullah Amin's dictatorial rule, the country was increasingly up in arms, galvanized by his revolutionary government's threat to their traditional social structures and Muslim faith. Within a few months of the 1978 'Saur Revolution' that had brought the PDPA to power, the first local risings would take place, with the March 1979 Herat revolt being crushed only through a massive air and ground attack that left thousands dead. Heavy-handed government reprisals only spurred on the rebels, whose numbers were also swollen by desertions from Kabul's forces. Amin proved increasingly dictatorial – he had his co-ruler Nur Mohammad Taraki arrested and then murdered – and refused to compromise.

Moscow tried and failed to persuade Amin to adopt a more moderate position, and increasingly feared that he would either spark a fundamentalist Islamic revolution – as had just happened in Iran – or turn to Washington for support. The Soviet invasion was thus expected to be a brief, limited operation: Operation *Storm-333*, a commando mission to eliminate Amin so he could be replaced by Babrak Karmal, who was regarded as both more moderate and less wilful, and Operation *Baikal-79*, a short, sharp demonstration of Soviet military power sufficient to stabilize the situation in the countryside.[2] Instead, it turned out to be just the start of a decade-long fight that the Soviets did not technically lose, but which it became clear they could not win, either.

This was a war fought as much in the air as on the ground. Indeed, arguably it was Soviet air power that made the difference between a defeat for Moscow, and the debilitating

1    See *The Soviet–Afghan War 1979–89* (Osprey Essential Histories 75, 2012)

2    See *Storm-333: KGB and Spetsnaz Seize Kabul, Soviet–Afghan War 1979* (Osprey RAID 54, 2021)

A Mil Mi-24D patrols the mountains near Kabul in April 1989. This was a Soviet gunship that was then transferred to the DRA during the withdrawal. (Derrick Ceyrac/AFP via Getty Images)

stalemate that reformist leader Mikhail Gorbachev eventually decided was no longer worth fighting. From the high-level bombing raids that blasted rebel-held mountain valleys, to the Mi-24 helicopter gunships and Su-25 jets that accompanied every substantial army operation, Soviet control of the air was a vital battlefield asset. It was as crucial for every aspect of its operations off the battlefield too, from the Mi-8 helicopters ferrying supplies to remote mountain-top observation points to An-12 'black tulips' taking the bodies of fallen soldiers on their last journey home.

Yet even if the rebel *mujahideen* had no air forces, this was not a wholly one-sided conflict. Even before they began to acquire man-portable surface-to-air missiles such as the controversial US FIM-92 Stinger, they adapted aggressively and imaginatively. They learnt new techniques of evasion, camouflage and deception, set up ambushes against low-level attacks, and even launched daring raids on airbases to destroy aircraft on the ground.

Drawing on both Russian and Western sources, this book explores and assesses rebel, Afghan government and Soviet operations, to paint a comprehensive picture of the air war over Afghanistan. Although even massive aerial superiority could not win this fight for the Soviets, nonetheless their experiences did revolutionize their understanding of air war, from the use of helicopters – a lesson the United States had likewise truly learnt in Vietnam – to the importance of giving pilots a degree of flexibility and freedom in their operations.

Afghanistan is, after all, an unforgiving combat environment, even for air forces. A Soviet General Staff assessment warned that, 'in terms of the nature of the terrain, Afghanistan is one of the most unfavourable of areas for aviation operations'. Some 70 per cent of the country is mountainous, with the mighty Hindu Kush range towering up to 7,000m in some cases, bisected by gorges of up to 3,000m depths. There were only five airfields with long enough runways for most modern combat aircraft – Kabul, Bagram, Jalalabad, Kandahar and Shindand – and they were all at altitude: 1,500–2,500m above sea level. In the high, thin air, helicopter rotors struggled to obtain sufficient lift, let alone negotiate what were often

**OPPOSITE** AFGHANISTAN AIRBASES

The Soviets built sometimes makeshift helicopter landing pads at all their bases, typically floored in corrugated metal sheets like this one at Baraki Barak in Logar Region, central-eastern Afghanistan. The crew of an Mi-8MT transport helicopter of the 50th OSAP in flight helmets, flanked by an Afghan civilian and two Soviet soldiers, pose for the camera in 1987. (E. Kuvakin/Vizu)

narrow passes, while the rugged relief scattered radio signals, confounded radar and provided no end of caves and dips in which rebels could hide or set ambushes. Even in the plains of the north and deserts of the south, spotting targets amidst rough, rocky scree was difficult, and without the kind of modern guidance systems still only just being introduced in Soviet aircraft, it was hard for pilots to orient themselves in the monotonous terrain.

It was not just about the relief but also the climate. In the icy winters, missions were often grounded by snowstorms and poor visibility, while the hot summers – when temperatures could go above 50 degrees centigrade – also saw air operations constrained by ground haze, sandstorms and high air temperatures. The metal skins of aircraft could heat up to fully 80 degrees under the scorching sun, with joins and seams potentially popping or distorting due to differential expansion, and dust storms could scour rotors, scratch the glass of cockpits and clog lubrication lines.

This would, in short, be a challenging battlefield for a Soviet Air Force that had been trained and equipped for conventional combat operations over the plains of northern Europe (or northern China). They – and the *mujahideen* so determined to drive the *Shuravi* ('Soviets') from their land – would have to learn its ways, and often paid a terrible price in doing so.

## Flying in an Afghan summer

One Soviet Mi-24 attack helicopter pilot based at Kandahar in the south, who flew two tours in the 280th Regiment, recalled the experience of having to fly in sandstorms as a particular terror: 'It's not just that visibility is so bad, it was that the sand choked the engine filters and even gnawed away at the rotor blades. Although it wasn't standard practice at the time, I would actually bribe my ground crew with *samogon* (homebrew alcohol) or anything else I could find to get them to clean out the filters fully after every flight so my engines didn't choke in mid-flight. We also had regularly to inspect the rotor blades, which got really pitted, and even the hydraulic systems risked getting jammed by the sand. It was a nightmare – whatever the challenges of flying in winter, I'd take them any day over high summer in Afghanistan.'

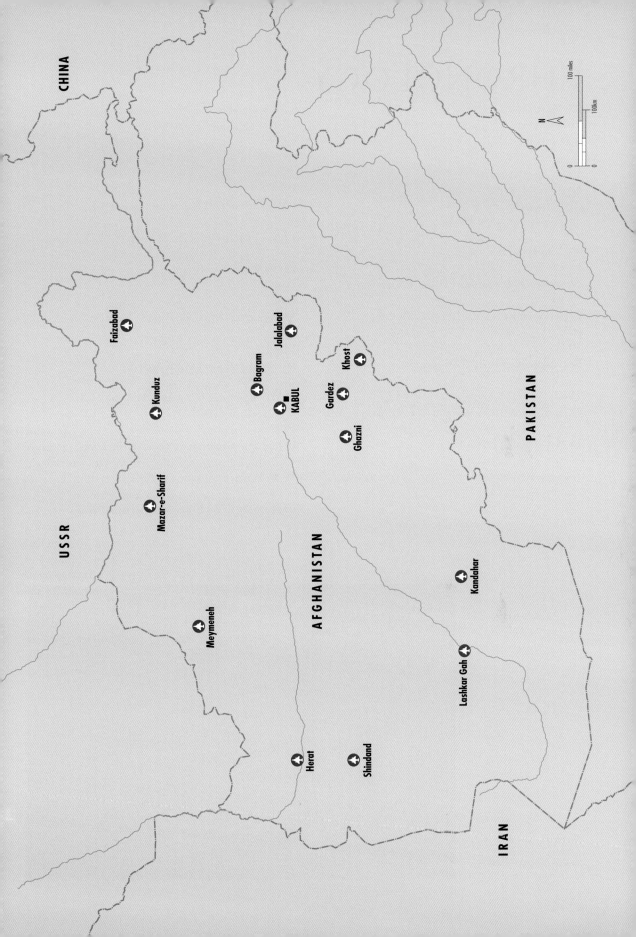

# CHRONOLOGY

**1979**
**27 December** Operations *Storm-333* and *Baikal-79*: Afghanistan invaded

**1980**
**March** Kunar Valley operation

**April–May** Operation *Rhombus*

**9–12 April** Panjshir I operation

**28 August–20 September** Panjshir II operation

**8–16 November** Panjshir III operation

**1981**
**6–11 September** Panjshir IV operation

**1982**
**25 April** Ahmad Shah Massoud raids Bagram

**16 May–1 June** Panjshir V operation

**28 August–10 September** Panjshir VI operation

**1984**
**19 April–5 May** Panjshir VII operation

**5–16 September** Panjshir VIII operation

**1985**
**16 June–16 July** Panjshir IX operation

**1986**
**4 May** Mohammad Najibullah replaces Babrak Karmal

**9 June–14 July** Operation *Manoeuvre*

**18–26 August** Operation *Trap*

**1987**
**23 November–10 January 1988** Operation *Highway*

**1988**
**14 April** Signing of Geneva Accords

**15 May** Beginning of Soviet withdrawal

**1989**
**20 January–4 February** Operation *Air-Bridge*

**23–26 January** Operation *Typhoon*

**15 February** Completion of Soviet withdrawal

An aerial view of winding roads in the Afghan foothills. (ZUMA Press Inc/Alamy)

# ATTACKER'S CAPABILITIES
## The Soviet Air Force in Afghanistan

The Soviet deployment to Afghanistan was known as the Limited Contingent of Soviet Forces in Afghanistan (OKSVA: *Ogranichenny Kontingent Sovietskikh Voisk v Afganistane*, sometimes simply rendered as OKSV), but the operational command was vested in the 40th Combined Arms Army. Initially, there was a distinct aerial command, the 34th Air Corps, but this was later made a subordinate element of the 40th Army once it became clear that this operation was not going to be the short, victorious deployment originally envisaged. The country was divided into four operational areas: North (including Kunduz, Mazar-e-Sharif and Faizabad), West (Shindand and Herat), East (Kabul, Bagram, Jalalabad and Khost) and South (Kandahar and Lashkar Gah). Each had its own sectoral command, reporting to the 40th Army staff.

Even if in many ways over-engineered for this kind of war, the Su-24M bomber demonstrated its effectiveness in Afghanistan. (Alexander Mishin)

Kabul airport on 31 December 1979, after the Soviet invasion. Note the cover over the front of the Mi-8 foreground, a necessity considering the harsh conditions of the Afghan winter. (François Lochon/Gamma-Rapho via Getty Images)

## Commanders of the 40th Army

| | |
|---|---|
| May 1979–23 Sept. 1980 | Lt General Yuri Tukharinov |
| 23 Sept. 1980–7 May 1982 | Lt General Boris Tkach |
| 7 May 1982–4 Nov. 1983 | Lt General Viktor Yermakov |
| 4 Nov. 1983–19 April 1985 | Lt General Leonid Generalov |
| 19 April 1985–30 April 1986 | Lt General Igor Rodionov |
| 30 April 1986–1 June 1987 | Lt General Viktor Dubynin |
| 1 June 1987–15 Feb. 1989 | Lt General Boris Gromov |

Direct authority of out-of-theatre forces such as strategic bombers and transport aviation was still vested in other structures such as the adjacent Turkestan Military District (TurkVO) and Long-Range Aviation (DA) command, and coordination would initially be something of an issue. However, as the General Staff increasingly put political capital into the war, it became clear that evidence of having been able to contribute to it was a useful entry in ambitious officers' service records. By around 1984, most accounts from veterans of the 40th Army command suggest that coordination worked rather more smoothly than they might have anticipated.

The 40th Army's aviation command was the 1325th Air Force Command Post in the capital, Kabul. The main air bases were at Kabul, Bagram north of Kabul, and Kandahar to the south, with smaller ones developed around the country over time in places such as Kunduz and Lashkar Gah. At first, many of these were very primitive encampments: veterans recalled shivering in tents and dugouts during the first winter of 1979–80, with neither hot water nor laundry facilities, so they had to live in the same clothes for days on end. Again, to a considerable extent this was simply because it was assumed that this would be a brief deployment, and commanders who all too often thought little of their men's comfort, regarded it as an acceptable short-term hardship. By winter 1980, however, proper field accommodation had been established, and the air bases became military cantonments with all the necessary facilities.

An Mi-8M helicopter returning to Kabul, after a mission to Baharak, Badakhshan province. (American Photo Archive/ Alamy)

## Rotor power

Just as Vietnam sealed the US military's love affair with the helicopter, so Afghanistan demonstrated to the Soviets its value in modern war in general, and counter-insurgencies in particular. There was scarcely any aspect of the 40th Army's operations in which helicopters did not play a crucial role, and the integration of the Army Aviation (AA: *Armeiskaya Aviatsiya*) branch of the 34th Air Corps into its command structure, with most units attached to specific brigades or divisions, proved to be very smooth.

Armed helicopters provided close air support for mechanized attacks, rapid responses to rebel ambushes, and both top cover for Soviet supply convoys and interdiction of *mujahideen* caravans. The most formidable source of mobile firepower was the Mi-24 'flying tank', an armoured gunship that could also carry eight soldiers, although in practice it usually added a couple of technicians as side-gunners to its regular complement of two crew. Although the DRA Air Force had received Mi-24 gunships before the invasion, the Soviets quickly scaled up their complement in Afghanistan and by the end of 1980, had fully 251 in-theatre. Rather than a lean attack ship like its US contemporary, the AH-1 Cobra, the Mi-24 was a heavyweight bruiser, with various versions equipped with bombs, rocket pods and missiles on its stub wings, as well as a gun, whether the Afanasev A-12.7 12.7mm machine-gun of the original model, the four-barrel 12.7mm Yakushev-Borzov Yak-B machine-gun of the widely deployed Mi-24D (Hind-D) and Mi-24V (Hind-E), or the fixed side-mounted 30mm GSh-30-2K twin-barrel autocannon of the later Mi-24P (Hind-F).[3]

| Soviet helicopters deployed in Afghanistan | | | | | | |
|---|---|---|---|---|---|---|
| Aircraft | Type | First flew | Crew | Weapons or cargo | Maximum range | Speed |
| Mi-6 (NATO: Hook) | Heavy transport | 1957 | 6 | 70 troops or 12,000kg; optional 12.7mm HMG | 970km | 300km/h |
| Mi-8T (NATO: Hip-C) | Medium transport | 1961 | 3 | 24 troops or 4,000kg; optional 4 rocket pods, 1–2 side-mounted MGs | 495km | 250km/h |
| Mi-8TVK (NATO: Hip-E) | Assault | 1961 | 3 | 12.7mm HMG, 6 hardpoints with bombs, rocket pods or four AT-2 ATGMs | 495km | 250km/h |
| Mi-24 (NATO: Hind-A) | Gunship | 1969 | 2–3 | 12.7mm HMG and rocket pods, gun pods, bombs or 4 ATGMs; optional 8 troops | 450km | 335km/h |
| Mi-24D (NATO: Hind-D) | Gunship | 1971 | 2–3 | 12.7mm Gatling HMG and rocket pods, gun pods, bombs or 4 ATGMs; optional 8 troops | 450km | 335km/h |
| Mi-24V (NATO: Hind-E) | Gunship | 1973 | 2–3 | 12.7mm Gatling HMG and rocket pods, gun pods, bombs or 8 ATGMs; optional 8 troops | 450km | 335km/h |
| Mi-24P (NATO: Hind-F) | Gunship | 1978 | 2–3 | 30mm twin-barrel autocannon and rocket pods, gun pods, bombs or 8 ATGMs; rarely 8 troops | 450km | 335km/h |

In the early years, Mi-24s would often fly at low altitudes, relying on their speed and armour to defeat rebel small arms fire, engaging targets with anti-tank guided missiles (ATGMs) at a range of 1,200–1,500m, unguided S-5 55mm rockets at around 1,000m and gunfire at

3    See *Mil Mi-24 Hind Gunship* (Osprey New Vanguard 171, 2012)

This head-on shot of a Mil-24, nicknamed the 'devil's chariot' by the *mujahideen*, demonstrates the sheer size of this gunship. (Patrick Aventurier/Gamma-Rapho via Getty Images)

700–900m. They also carried a range of explosive or incendiary bombs, especially for use against fortified targets, as well as the KGMU 2V mine dispenser pod. Later, as the threat from rebel AA guns and MANPADS (man-portable air defence systems) became more severe, they not only learnt new tactics but also acquired more countermeasures, including flare dispensers to decoy heat-seeking missiles, and baffles to reduce the heat signature of their exhausts.

Although Mi-24s were occasionally used in their original role as 'flying IFVs', the rugged and versatile Mi-8 was the real workhorse, whether as a troop carrier, supply truck or even assault ship. A design dating back to the late 1950s, which first flew in 1961, the Mi-8 was originally developed for the civilian market, but was belatedly taken up by the military as a troop carrier, able to lift 24 fully equipped soldiers or 3 tonnes in stores. The basic Mi-8T/Mi-8MT (NATO codename 'Hip-C') was usually unarmed, but could carry four rocket pods on outrigger pylons, and would increasingly also have one or two door-gunners manning 7.62mm PK machine guns. The Mi-8TVK (Hip-E) assault version mounted a 12.7mm KV-4 machine gun in the nose and rocket pods, bombs or four 3M11 *Fleyta* (AT-2 Swatter) ATGMs on outriggers.

However, its real value was its versatility as a platform for a wide range of specialist missions. The Mi-8MB *Bissektrisa* (Bisector) medevac (medical evacuation) ambulance lifted

## The reconnaissance-strike mission

The need to interdict rebel supply caravans as part of Plan Veil, as well as limit the activity of their raiding parties, led the Soviets to adopt the Reconnaissance-Strike Action (RUD: *Razvedyvatelno-Udarnye Dyeystviya*). This was generally carried out by a pair (sometimes two pairs) of helicopters, usually the better-armed Mi-24s, but occasionally with Mi-8s in support. Sometimes, they operated simply on general principles, but more often working on the basis of intelligence gathered by the KhAD or Soviet aerial reconnaissance. The helicopters would quarter their patrol area at an altitude of 1,500–1,700m, maintaining an interval of 600–800m, to give them maximum visibility and freedom of manoeuvre, while still being able to support each other. Upon identifying a suspicious caravan, whether of vehicles or pack mules or horses, they would fire warning shots to make it stop. One helicopter would land an inspection team – this was one of the relatively few situations where the Mi-24's troop-carrying capacity was employed in Afghanistan – then lift again to take up overwatch. If the caravan failed to stop, or opened fire on the helicopters or the inspection team, then it would be destroyed from the air. Too often, especially in the later stages of the war, RUDs adopted a 'shoot first, check the burnt-out vehicles later' approach, especially in areas of heavy *mujahideen* activity. Nonetheless, the RUDs, while winning the *Shuravi* few friends in the local population, did represent an effective means of constraining the rebels' supply operations and general freedom of movement.

The Mil Mi-6 heavy-lift helicopter was a powerful asset, but its vulnerability was such that after the first few losses, it was banned from carrying soldiers, until this edict was relaxed at the end of the war. (aviation-images.com/ Universal Images Group via Getty Images)

the wounded from the battlefield, while commanders would oversee operations from the Mi-8VKP aerial command post, the Mi-8AV scattered mines and so on. In the words of one former staff officer of the 40th Army, 'the Mi-8 may not be as well known outside *Afgan*, but to me, it was perhaps the most indispensable weapon of the war'.

Although the first year of the war saw occasional use of the Mi-10 flying crane, the biggest beast in the Soviet fleet was the massive Mi-6, the largest helicopter in the world until it was replaced by the Mi-26. At the peak, there were perhaps 60 deployed in Afghanistan, including a unit formally part of the DRA forces but with Soviet crews. Two heavy-lift battalions were rotated between Bagram, Kabul, Kandahar, Kunduz and Shindand as operational needs

The Soviet state would, in effect, 'conscript' whatever it needed, like these civilian Aeroflot Mi-8 helicopters used to bring troops into Kabul airport in January 1980. (Hans Paul/Lehtikuva/AFP via Getty Images)

dictated. Although able to carry troops, ammunition or even vehicles, one of its most crucial roles was delivering food to outposts in locations where the geography or the density of rebel forces made land convoys too dangerous. For over a year, for example, an Mi-6 battalion based in Kunduz flew almost daily resupply flights to stations in Bamyan Province, north-west of Kabul. Its size meant it officially needed at least 350m of runway to take off or land, but in practice pilots often flouted the regulations, learning how to 'dance' their bulky charges up from shorter stretches.

A Separate Helicopter Aviation Regiment (OVP: *Otdelny Vertolyotny Aviatsionny Polk*) comprised three or four 12-ship squadrons, typically a mix of Mi-24 and Mi-8, although as the value of helicopters became clearer, some expanded further. In 1982, for example, the 181st OVP acquired a fifth squadron, which was based at Maymana. There were also independent forces, typically each a stand-alone Separate Helicopter Aviation Squadron (OVE: *Otdelnaya Vertolotnaya Eskadrilya*). These had particular roles. The 205th and 239th OVEs flying out of Jalalabad and Lashkar Gah, for example, were directly assigned to supporting *Spetsnaz* special force operations.

| Army aviation units in Afghanistan | | | | |
|---|---|---|---|---|
| Airbase | Unit | Aircraft | Deployment | Notes |
| Kabul | 290th OVP | Mi-8, Mi-24 | 1979–89 | |
| | 339th OVP | Mi-8, Mi-24 | 1980–89 | |
| Bagram | 338th OVP | Mi-8, Mi-24 | 1980–89 | |
| | 262nd OVE | Mi-8, Mi-24 | 1981–89 | Attached to 201st Division |
| Jalalabad | 292nd OVP | Mi-8, Mi-24 | 1980–81 | |
| | 335th OVP | Mi-8, Mi-24 | 1981–89 | Replaced 292nd OVP |
| | 208th OVE | Mi-8, Mi-24 | 1982–88 | |
| Kandahar | 280th OVP | Mi-6, Mi-8, Mi-24 | 1979–89 | Attached to 70th Brigade |
| | 289th OVP | Mi-8, Mi-24 | 1980–88 | |
| Kunduz | 181st OVP | Mi-6, Mi-8MT, Mi-24 | 1979–89 | Five squadrons after 1982 |
| | 292nd OVP | Mi-6, Mi-8, Mi-24 | N/A | Attached to 66th Independent Motor Rifle Brigade |
| | 146th OVE | Mi-8, Mi-24 | 1980–89 | 1980, attached to 201st Division |
| | 254th OVE | Mi-8, Mi-24 | N/A | Attached to 201st Division |
| Lashkar Gah | 205th OVE | Mi-8MT, Mi-24 | N/A | Attached to 22nd *Spetsnaz* Brigade |
| | 239th OVE | Mi-8MT, Mi-24 | 1986–88 | Rotated between Lashkar Gah and Ghazni |
| Shindand | 302nd OVE | Mi-8, Mi-24 | 1979–89 | Attached to 5th Division |

## Close air support

While helicopter gunships were appreciated for their capacity to loiter in support of ground operations, the ground-attack aircraft assigned to the 40th Army by Frontal Aviation (FA: *Frontovaya Aviatsiya*), one of the separate Soviet Air Force commands, performed an equally significant role. The iconic aircraft of the war was the Su-25 *Grach* (Rook, NATO codename 'Frogfoot'), an armoured, dedicated ground-attack aircraft designed as a spiritual successor to the Il-2 *Shturmovik* of World War II.[4] It was rugged, heavily armed with a 30mm GSh-30-2 cannon and almost 4.5 tonnes of bombs, rockets, missiles or gunpods, and its relatively slow minimum speed compared to the rest of the fixed-wing FA arsenal meant it could be more accurate and operate in tighter operational environments. It could also safely engage targets from lower altitudes – often just 500–1,000m, compared to 2,000–2,500m for fighters pressed into ground attack work – with all the advantages this meant for accuracy. No wonder a senior OKSVA commander called it 'the Kalashnikov of the air fleet – the one weapon you could always rely on'.

| Soviet tactical aircraft in Afghanistan | | | | | | |
|---|---|---|---|---|---|---|
| Aircraft | Type | First flew | Crew | Armament | Maximum range | Speed |
| MiG-21 (NATO: Fishbed) | Fighter | 1955 | 1 | 1 x 23mm gun; 5 x hardpoints | 1,670km | 2,175km/h |
| MiG-21bis (NATO: Fishbed-L) | Fighter | 1957 | 1 | 1 x 23mm gun; 4 x hardpoints | 1,210km | 2,175km/h |
| MiG-23 (NATO: Flogger) | Fighter | 1967 | 1 | 1 x 23mm gun; 6 x hardpoints | 1,500km | 2,499km/h |
| MiG-27 (Flogger-D) | Ground Attack | 1970 | 1 | 1 x 30mm gun; 7 x hardpoints | 780km | 1,885km/h |
| Su-17 (NATO: Fitter) | Swing-wing fighter-bomber | 1966 | 1 | 2 x 30mm cannon; 12 x hardpoints for 4,000kg ordnance | 1,150km | 1,860km/h |
| Su-25 (NATO: Frogfoot) | Ground Attack | 1975 | 1 | 1 x 30mm cannon; 11 x hardpoints for 4,400kg ordnance | 1,000km | 975km/h |

However, the full range of other fighter-bombers in Soviet service also saw action in Afghanistan, along with some fighters which were deployed because of early fears that the

4    See *Sukhoi Su-25 Frogfoot* (Osprey Air Vanguard 9, 2013)

The Su-25 *Grach* earned the fear of the rebels and the respect of the Soviets for its firepower, especially using rockets, as here. (Nikolay Doychinov/ AFP via Getty Images)

A MiG-21 in the silver colour scheme used for interceptors, on display at the National Air and Space Museum Steven F. Udvar-Hazy Center in Chantilly, Virginia. (Balon Greyjoy)

USA or its ally Pakistan might directly intervene. While there were some engagements with the Pakistani Air Force, in practice they were more often used on a limited basis for ground-attack missions, even though their capacities in that role were relatively limited. A number of MiG-21PFM (NATO: Fishbed-F) interceptors were sent to Kabul, for example, but although they could carry gunpods with 23mm GSh-23 cannon, or bombs or Kh-66 air-to-surface missiles on two underwing pylons, they were quickly withdrawn in March 1980 as unsuited to this mission and replaced by the MiG-21SM (Fishbed-J) and MiG-21bis (Fishbed-L/N), which at least had internal cannon, as well as scope to carry an external fuel tank to increase its range.

Fighter aircraft were not especially well suited to attacking small, scattered targets, often in rough terrain. They could not carry heavy bombs – or many of them – nor were their pilots especially trained in using their guns in such circumstances, especially as they were flying at relatively high speeds. MiG-21s, for example, typically carried just two FAB-250 bombs, because in the hot and high environments in which they were operating, they needed to keep their loaded weight to a minimum.

Subsequently, the MiG-21s were succeeded by more modern MiG-23ML/MLD variable-geometry fighters, which had better avionics and could carry more ordnance and, at the very end of the war, MiG-27D fighter-bombers. These were more capable but again designed

# Bombing approaches

Soviet pilots developed a range of signature attack patterns best suited to operations against rebels on foot or horseback, typically operating in rough terrain.

**Pair Dive Strike:** Generally used in the tight environs of mountain valleys, where there was less scope for lateral manoeuvres and the goal was to deliver a quick strike before the rebels could disperse into cover, this entailed the leader diving into the attack at a 30- to 40-degree angle and releasing bombs or firing rockets at the lowest practical altitude before pulling up. His wingman would follow, at enough of an interval to allow last-minute corrections to targeting, but otherwise as quickly as possible.

**Carousel:** Aircraft, ideally in larger numbers, took it in turns to make their attack run, keeping the target under constant attack. This was often used against concentrations of rebel troops in more open areas, not least because it demanded careful coordination.

**Cabriolet:** Experienced crews could use this method against known, fixed targets, allowing a degree of indirect fire, even over intervening terrain. The aircraft accelerated in a gentle descent, then turned up to a 30- or even 45-degree angle, releasing its bombs at the top of its climb, before banking to one side. The bomb could, depending on the speed and angle of separation, fly for several kilometres to the target

**Night Strike:** The lead aircraft dropped parachute flares from an altitude of 2,000–3,000m onto the anticipated target. These so-called 'chandeliers' would burn for 6–8 minutes, giving time for the wingman to then attack with guns, rockets or bombs from a range of 1,500–2,000m. In rare cases, an especially quick-manoeuvring (and confident) leader might be able to loop round and still have time to make an attack run of his own.

for conventional war in Europe rather than counter-insurgency and operations in tight mountain passes.

Even so, the real teeth of the FA in Afghanistan were the Su-25 and the older Su-17 fighter-bomber, a rugged swing-wing fighter-bomber that is still in service today. They were used for reconnaissance missions, but more often in the direct attack role, whether as part of pre-planned strike missions or 'free hunting'. In the latter missions, they would be assigned an area to patrol and could engage – sometimes only on being given permission by their command, at other times, at will – targets of opportunity they encountered, typically rebel caravans.

A comparative array of Soviet ordnance: from left to right, the RBK-250 cluster bomb, OFAB-250-270 fragmentation bomb, FAB-500 M54 high-drag high explosive bomb. (George Chernilevsky)

Aircraft typically operated in pairs. A single pair would usually be deployed for reconnaissance or battle damage assessment missions, or to designate a target for air or artillery attack. One or two pairs (known as a 'link') would undertake air defence suppression, and two to four pairs a full strike mission. On rare occasions, a full 12-aircraft squadron might be deployed, but typically no more than ten were operational at any one time.

FA units were rotated through Afghanistan more rapidly than many other air force elements. In total, 11 Fighter Aviation Regiments (IAP: *Istrebitelny Aviatsionny Polk*), one Separate Attack Aviation Regiment (OShAP: *Otdelny Shturmovy Aviatsionny Polk*), one Separate Attack Aviation Squadron (OShAE: *Otdelnaya Shturmovaya Aviatsionnaya Eskadrilya*) and seven Fighter-Bomber Aviation Regiments (IBAP: *Istrebitelno-Bombardirovochny Aviatsionny Polk*) would rotate through the OKSVA. The aggressive and consistent use of FA aircraft is also evident in their losses through the course of the war: 21 MiG-21s, 11 MiG-23s, 34 Su-17s (including Su-22s, its export version) and 36 Su-25s.

| Frontal aviation units rotated through Afghanistan | | | |
|---|---|---|---|
| Unit | Airbase | Aircraft | Deployment |
| 27th IAP | Shindand | MiG-21UB | 1981–82 |
| 115th IAP | Bagram, Kandahar | MiG-22bis | 1979–81 |
| 120th IAP | Bagram | MiG-23MLD, MiG-23UB | 1988–89 |
| 145th IAP | Kandahar | MiG-21bis | 1982–83 |
| 168th IAP | Bagram | MiG-23MLD, MiG-23UB | 1986–87 |
| 190th IAP | Bagram | MiG-23MLD | 1986–88 |
| 655th IAP | Bagram | MiG-23MLD | 1985–86 |
| 905th IAP | Bagram | MiG-23MLD | 1984–85 |
| 927th IAP | Kandahar | MiG-21bis | 1983–84 |
| 979th IAP | Kandahar | MiG-23MLD | 1986–89 |
| 982nd IAP | Kandahar | MiG-23MLD | 1984–86 |
| 134th IBAP | Shindand | MiG-27 | 1988–89 |
| 136th IBAP | Kabul, Bagram, Kandahar | Su-17M3 | N/A |
| 156th IBAP | Mary-2 (USSR), later Kandahar | Su-17M3 | N/A |
| 166th IBAP | Kandahar | Su-17M3 | N/A |
| 168th IBAP | Khanabad (USSR) | Su-17M3 | N/A |
| 217th IBAP | Shindand | Su-17M4 | N/A |
| 274th IBAP | Bagram | Su-17M4 | N/A |
| 378th OShAP | Bagram, Shindand | Su-25 | 1984–89 |
| 200th OShAE | Shindand | Su-25 | 1981–84 |

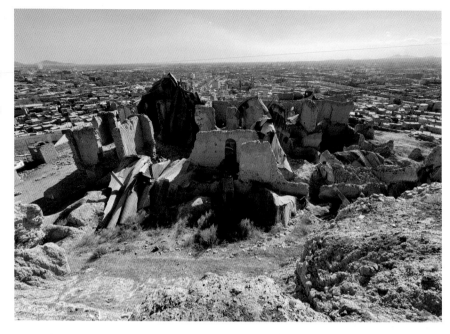

Bala Hissar, residence of Turkish sultan Mahmud of Ghazni, known as the Conqueror of India, who lived between AD 971 and 1030. This historic site in Ghazni has been ruined by the successive wars fought in Afghanistan, from the 1980s to the 2020s. (Mustafa Melih Ahishali/ Anadolu Agency via Getty Images)

# Bombing

The airfields of the Soviet Turkestan and Central Asian Military Districts would increasingly become the bases from which long-range bombing raids were launched into Afghanistan by both the Su-24 tactical bomber – which was also part of Frontal Aviation's fleet – and the strategic bombers of Long-Range Aviation (DA: *Dalnaya Aviatsiya* or Bomber Command). This title will be used throughout, even though in 1980 it was briefly renamed the 37th Air Army of Strategic Purpose of the Supreme High Command, before its original title was returned to it in 1988.

The Su-24, a supersonic, all-weather swing-wing multi-role fighter-bomber proved in some ways too capable to be of much use in Afghanistan. It was reliable and could carry a wide range of ordnance, including bombs, air-to-air and air-to-ground missiles and reconnaissance pods, to a total load of 7,000kg (although the usual load was closer to 4,000kg). It was also the first Soviet combat aircraft to be equipped with the *Puma* integrated digital navigation and day/night attack system, that allowed it to strike targets with a greater degree of precision. However, unlike the Su-25, it flew too fast to allow its crew to target anything but especially large and pre-plotted targets. It had its combat debut in 1984, in support of major combined-arms operations against the Panjshir Valley stronghold of rebel field commander Ahmad Shah Massoud.[5] A squadron of Su-24s was used to carpet-bomb known and suspected defensive positions along the axis of the attack. At that time, they dropped mixes of 1,500kg and 500kg bombs from a height of 5,000m but as the rebels acquired increasingly sophisticated MANPADS, they were forced to operate at higher altitudes, typically up to 8,000m, and accuracy suffered as a result.

Although sometimes staged out of Khanabad airbase, the three Bomber Aviation Regiments (BAP: *Bombardirovochnny Aviatsionny Polk*) involved in the war at different times – the 143rd BAP from Kutaisi-1, the 149th Guards BAP from Alma-Ata and the 735th BAP from Qarshi – were generally not permanently based inside Afghanistan. Instead, their Su-24 units were

5    See *The Panjshir Valley, 1980–86* (Osprey Campaign 369, 2021)

drawn from TurkVO's 73rd Air Army and largely operated out of Kokaity airbase outside Tashkent in Uzbekistan. They continued to fly through the war – especially in supporting the eventual withdrawal of the 40th Army – and even after, they were kept on standby for a few months later in case there was an immediate assault on Kabul and they needed to support DRA forces.

Long-Range Aviation's contribution to the war effort involved Tu-16, Tu-22M2 and Tu-22M3 bombers, which generally also flew out of bases in the Soviet Union. Again, this was not really the kind of war for which these aircraft had been designed and for which their crews – at least at first – had been trained. They were, after all, really meant for the destruction of static, strategic targets; given the rebels' mobility and usual dispersed deployment, they were primarily used against known *mujahideen* bases, including cave complexes, and to clear areas in advance of ground attacks.

| Soviet bombers in Afghanistan | | | | | | |
| --- | --- | --- | --- | --- | --- | --- |
| Aircraft | Type | First flew | Crew | Warload | Maximum range | Speed |
| Tu-16 (NATO: Badger) | Strategic bomber | 1952 | 6 | 9,000kg bombs | 7,200km | 1,050km/h |
| Tu-22M2 (NATO: Backfire-B) | Supersonic bomber | 1969 | 4 | 24,000kg bombs | 6,800km | 1,997km/h |
| Tu-22M3 (NATO: Backfire-C) | Supersonic bomber | 1977 | 4 | 24,000kg bombs | 6,800km | 1,997km/h |

To this end, initially they were used quite sparingly, largely against targets in the Panjshir Valley. A turning point was the 1984 Panjshir operations when Tu-16 and Tu-22M2 bombers were used for high-altitude raids at heights of up to 10,000m. They were deemed to have underperformed, because the bombs they used were often dated designs and had only limited blast radii, and also because crews too often demonstrated poor technical skills and commitment to the operation. One former Tu-22M2 crewman openly admitted: 'In the early days, we had no real idea what was going on in *Afgan*, and what our boys were facing. We treated it just as casually as a training operation.'

This would change, though, and from late 1985 or early 1986, DA bombers were being used more frequently and with a greater appreciation of what they could and

The massive 9-tonne FAB-9000 M-54 demolition bomb was only used late in the war, and it had as much a psychological as a practical effect. (Viktor Kuzmin)

could not do. In particular, for example, they were used against cave complexes and other especially hard targets. Their valley-side locations and construction made them relatively difficult to target and damage with the lighter bombs used by close-air support aircraft, but the larger ones the heavy bombers could drop, not least the 5-tonne FAB-5000NG, could crack stone, collapse roofs and bury openings in avalanches. At the same time, DA crews apparently began taking their missions more seriously, because of both growing awareness of the nature of the war and increased pressure from the command structure. In 1986, a captain serving at Mary-2 airbase in Soviet Turkmenistan was even prosecuted for dereliction of duty for choosing to go drinking rather than attend a debriefing intended to improve the accuracy of air missions over Afghanistan – he had not realised that the commander of the TurkVO's air forces had decided to attend.

The swing-wing, supersonic Tu-22M2 and refined Tu-22M3 saw their first combat use in Afghanistan, and like most of the DA assets operational in the war, were based at Mary-2 airbase in Turkmenistan. There was also a single Heavy Bomber Aviation Regiment (TBAP: *Tyazholy Bombardirovochny Aviatsionny Polk*) at Mary-1 and another, the 200th Guards at Khanabad even if it sometimes staged out of bases in northern Afghanistan. These units had been drawn from across the USSR and would be heavily reinforced during the 1988–89 endgame in order to support the withdrawal of the 40th Army. They could target any location across Afghanistan, and operated high enough to be safe from any *mujahideen* air defences. None were lost to combat or accident throughout the war (though one Su-24 was lost in December 1988 when it skidded off the runway at Karshi airfield in Soviet Uzbekistan on coming in to land).

| Long-Range Aviation units active over Afghanistan | | | | |
|---|---|---|---|---|
| Airbase | Unit | Aircraft | Drawn from | Deployment |
| Khanabad | 200th Guards TBAP | Tu-16 | Bobruisk | 1984–88 |
| Mary-1 | 251st Guards TBAP | Tu-16 | Belaya Tserkov | 1988–89 |
| Mary-2 | 52nd TBAP | Tu-22M3 | Shaikovka | 1988–89 |
| | 185th Guards TBAP | Tu-22M3 | Poltava | 1985–89 |
| | 341st TBAP | Tu-22M3 | Ozernoye | 1988–89 |
| | 402nd TBAP | Tu-22M3 | Orsha | 1988–89 |
| | 1225th TBAP | Tu-22M2 | Belaya | 1985–89 |
| | 840th TBAP | Tu-22M3 | Novgorodskiye Soltsy | 1988–89 |

# Airlift

The difficult relief of Afghanistan and the rebels' talent for ambushes meant that, while the roads were still the main arteries for major movements of troops and supplies, airlift was essential for rapid and – relatively – safe transports in, from and around the country. Beyond the helicopters used for tactical lift, this meant the fixed-wing aircraft of Military Transport Aviation (VTA: *Voyennaya Transportnaya Aviatsiya*), supplemented by more from the state airline Aeroflot, with military crews.

Over the ten years of the war, the VTA made some 27,000 flights, with the frequency rising from 150–200 a month to 400–500 at the peak of operations. They transported more than 880,000 personnel and 430,000 tonnes of cargo. Increasingly, this would be in the face of enemy attacks, especially by gunfire and missiles fired by *mujahideen* in concealed positions near airbases, so as to catch aircraft on take-off or landing. The

Even transport aircraft were fitted with flare dispensers to try to protect them during their vulnerable take-offs and landings. (Robert Nickelsberg/Getty Images)

Soviets lost two Il-76, eight An-12 and five An-26 from accidents and enemy action, and 1,700 VTA personnel were decorated for their service. The basic element was the 50th Separate Mixed Aviation Regiment (OSAP: *Otdelny Smeshanny Aviatsionny Polk*) in Kabul, which also included Mi-24 gunships used to escort transport flights, along with Military Transport Aviation Regiments (VTAP: *Voyenny Transportny Aviatsionny Polk*) based over the border in the USSR.

| Soviet transport aircraft | | | | | | |
|---|---|---|---|---|---|---|
| Aircraft | Type | First flew | Crew | Cargo | Maximum range | Speed |
| An-12 (NATO: Cub) | Medium-range cargo and paratrooper transport | 1957 | 5 | 60 troops or 20,000kg | 5,700km | 660km/h |
| An-22 Antei (NATO: Cock) | Heavy transport | 1965 | 5 | 80,000kg | 10,950km | 740km/h |
| An-24 (NATO: Coke) | Tactical transport | 1959 | 3 | 50 troops | 2,400km | 500km/h |
| An-26 (NATO: Curl) | Light tactical transport | 1969 | 5 | 40 troops or 5,500kg | 2,500km | 540km/h |
| Il-76 (NATO: Candid) | Strategic transport | 1971 | 5 | 140 troops or 42,000kg | 4,000km | 900km/h |

Although the An-22 had a greater capacity, the Il-76 was the workhorse of Soviet strategic airlift, carrying almost 90 per cent of all military personnel flown in or out of the country, and 74 per cent of all freight. With a service ceiling of some 15km, it was only vulnerable on landing and take-off, but it also proved rugged enough often to be able to shrug off machine-gun fire and even some hits by MANPADS. The smaller An-26, though, was in many ways an unhailed star of the VTA's operations in Afghanistan. This high-wing, two-engine turboprop could use improvised runways when need be, was expressly designed for quick unloading and sported a Tumansky Ru-19-A300 turbojet in the right engine nacelle for an additional boost. This not only allowed it to climb quickly out of rebel anti-air range but also helped it operate in 'hot and high' conditions.

The scale of the Il-76 heavy lifter – as well as the 23mm cannons in a tail turret – is made clear by this photo of Ural-4320 trucks being unloaded. (USAF)

| Military transport aviation units in Afghanistan | | | | |
|---|---|---|---|---|
| Airbase | Unit | Aircraft | Drawn from | Deployment |
| Kabul | 50th OSAP | An-12, An-26RR, An-30B, An-26, Mi-8MT, Mi-24D | | 1979–89 |
| | 224th OATO | An-12 | | |
| Bagram | Squadron of 930th VTAP | An-12 | Tashkent | |
| Meymana | 339th OSAE | An-26, Mi-8MT | | 1988–89 |
| Units based in USSR | | | | |
| Tashkent | 930th VTAP | An-12 | Tashkent, Fergana | 1979–89 |
| | 111th OSAP | An-12, An-26, Mi-6 | Tashkent | 1980–88 |
| Fergana | 194th VTAP | An-12BP, Il-76 | Fergana | 1985–89 |
| Panevezhis | 128th VTAP | Il-76 | Panevezhis | 1979–89 |

# Supporting the war

In counter-insurgency, knowledge is victory, and because of the frequent difficulties the KGB and their Afghan KhAD (later WAD) counterparts had penetrating many rebel units, the role of the air force in mapping the battlespace and monitoring rebel movements was often invaluable.

The An-30B, a specialized version of the An-24 tactical transport fitted with multiple cameras for aerial cartography, was used from 1982 to map Afghanistan in detail, allowing the Soviets to plot air attacks, artillery fires and ground operations with greater accuracy than their old 1960s-vintage maps would allow. One was shot down by a SA-7 MANPADS south of the Panjshir Valley in March 1985. It was hit in the left engine, and while most of its seven-man crew bailed out successfully, the pilot and co-pilot tried to land at Bagram

airport, but fire spread to the control services and it crashed some 25km from Kabul and both were killed. After this, the remaining models were fitted with flare and chaff dispensers.

As well as MiG-21R and Su-17M3R reconnaissance versions of the 263rd detachment, flying out of Kabul and Bagram, the Soviets also deployed flights out of bases inside their own territory. Su-24R reconnaissance aircraft flew out of Kokaity, both to locate targets and carry out after-action battle damage assessments. Furthermore, they deployed Yak-28Rs, a

A Soviet Antonov An-22 coming in to land at Kabul airport during the early stage of the invasion. (Bettmann/Contributor via Getty Images)

Although these days Moscow generally seeks to take what glory it can from past wars, the Afghan War was a Soviet one which took the lives of men and women of every constituent nationality. This is a memoriul to soldiers fallen during the war in Izmail, south-western Ukraine. (Yakudza/CC-BY-SA-4.0)

**OPPOSITE** MILITARY-MEDICAL AIRLIFT NETWORK

modified version of a medium bomber with the NATO codename 'Brewer-D', fitted with an Initsiativa-2 radar, and five interchangeable modules with various types of camera or the Romb-4A radio-location suite.

More broadly, air assets were used in every aspect of operations. While also used to take the dead back home (see box), they also had a key role in the casualty evacuation and military medical process, something of a first for a Soviet military which for so long had treated its men often as so much human ammunition. Once evacuated from the battlefield, An-26 Spasitel (Saviour) light medical transports would often take the wounded to military hospitals in-country, while for those who were being sent to higher-order facilities back in the USSR, Il-16 Sanitar (Orderly) and Il-76 Skalpel (Scalpel) or regular Tu-154 passenger aircraft would take them either to Tashkent or Moscow.

## The DRA Air Force

Soviet assistance to the Afghan Air Force went back all the way to 1925, when the USSR began to provide assistance to the Royal Air Force of Afghanistan, often in competition with the British, a rivalry the Afghans artfully encouraged to get both sides to provide aircraft and training. Although Soviet–Afghan relations went through their ups and downs, by the 1950s the USSR had established itself as the main source of military assistance. When the monarchy was toppled in a coup in 1973, the new republican government under Mohammed Daoud Khan maintained friendly relations with Moscow. The air force remained a particular beneficiary of Soviet assistance, including training in its academies and flight schools. To Moscow, this was also a means of winning over the Afghan military and it is certainly true that the relatively better-educated air force tended to be much more pro-Soviet in its outlook.

Nonetheless, the overall levels of education did prove something of a problem to the DRA Air Force, especially in filling other ranks' positions. Reportedly, before the invasion, General Gausuddin, commander of the DRA Air Force, was travelling across the country with a visiting delegation of Soviet officers, when they stopped to watch a passing nomadic caravan. He turned to his Soviet counterparts and said: 'Your children are born to the noise of the TV, and even before they learn how to speak, they already know how to turn on the light and the tape recorder, or turn the steering wheel of the car. When they grow up, they are not afraid to break away from one control knob and grab another. And our children come off the tail of a donkey or a camel, from their mother's skirts, and you want to put him right into the cockpit of a modern aircraft? Don't push and don't rush.'

This may have been a fair comment, but the increasing challenge of rural insurrection meant that the DRA had to push and rush. By the time of the 'Saur Revolution' staged by the PDPA in 1978, the Afghan Air Force had some 180 aircraft in service, although a number were not airworthy. These were essentially Moscow's hand-me-downs, older

## The Black Tulip and Cargo 200s

A particular ritual and mythology grew up around the so-called 'Black Tulips', the dedicated An-12 transport aircraft that brought 'Cargo 200s' (the military code designation for fatalities) back to the Soviet Union. (The 'Black Tulip' even had songs about it.) The service got its name from the logo of the funeral company in Tashkent that made the zinc-lined coffins that were used by the OKSVA, with up to 15 on each flight. Each coffin would usually be accompanied by a friend of the dead soldier or an officer from his unit, who would then join the official party from the local *voyenkomat* military commissariat, which would notify the next of kin.

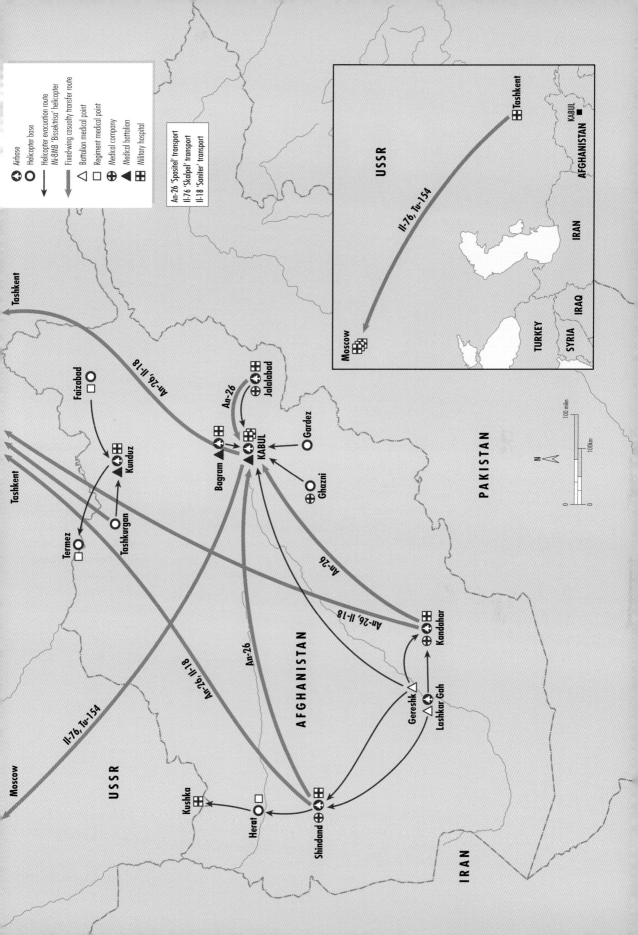

**Legend:**

- ✈ Airbase
- ◯ Helicopter base
- → Helicopter evacuation route — Mi-8MB 'Bissektrisa' helicopter
- ⟹ Fixed-wing casualty transfer route

- △ Battalion medical point
- ▢ Regiment medical point
- ⊕ Medical company
- ▲ Medical battalion
- ⊞ Military hospital

An-26 'Spasitel' transport
Il-76 'Skalpel' transport
Il-18 'Sanitar' transport

**Inset map (top right):**

USSR — Tashkent ⊞ — Il-76, Tu-154 — Moscow ⊞

KABUL ■
AFGHANISTAN
IRAN
TURKEY
SYRIA
IRAQ

**Main map labels:**

Tashkent

USSR

Moscow
Il-76, Tu-154

Kushka ⊞

Herat ◯
Shindand ⊕ ⊞ ✈

Faizabad ▢ ◯

Kunduz ⊞ ✈ ▲

Termez ◯ ▢

Tashkurgan ◯

Bagram ▲ ⊞ ✈

Jalalabad ⊞ ✈ ⊕

KABUL ⊞ ✈ ▲

Gardez ◯

Ghazni ⊕ ◯

An-26

An-26, Il-18

An-26, Il-18

An-26

Gereshk △
Lashkar Gah △ ✈

Kandahar ⊞ ✈ ⊕

AFGHANISTAN

PAKISTAN

IRAN

N

100 miles
100km

Soviet patronage predated the PDPA's revolution as is shown by this photo of Afghan Air Force Mikoyan-Gurevich MiG-15 fighters and Ilyushin Il-28 bombers in Kabul during a visit by US president Dwight D. Eisenhower in December 1959. (Sovfoto/Universal Images Group via Getty Images)

aircraft no longer in front-line Soviet service, including 86 1950s-vintage MiG-17 fighters and 24 Su-7BMK fighter-bombers and 24 of the even older Il-28 light bombers. Some 28 MiG-21 supersonic fighters represented the most modern airframes at Kabul's disposal. In total, the DRA Air Force had six regiments, to which another, the 7th Separate Helicopter Regiment, was later added when the Soviets also provided them with rotor-wing assets. This sufficed for Afghanistan's defensive needs, but would prove of rather limited value in the counter-insurgency operations that followed the outbreak of rebellion.

| DRA Air Force, mid-1979 | | |
|---|---|---|
| Base | Unit | Aircraft |
| Kabul | 373rd Transport Aviation Regiment | An-26, Il-14 |
| | Flight Technical School | |
| Bagram | 322nd Aviation Regiment | MiG-17, MiG-21 |
| | 355th Aviation Regiment | Su-7BMK |
| | 7th Helicopter Regiment | Mi-4, Mi-8, Mi-25 |
| | Aircraft Repair Plant | |
| Kandahar | 366th Aviation Regiment | MiG-17 |
| Mazar-e-Sharif | 393rd Training Aviation Regiment | L-39 |
| Shindand | 335th Aviation Regiment | An-2, An-30, Il-28, MiG-17, Su-7 |

In 1978, the Soviets provided Kabul with 18 Mi-24 helicopter gunships, later followed by another squadron of 18 Mi-24Ds the following year. They also began upgrading its fixed-wing fleet. In December 1978, Moscow had promised gradually to replace the Su-7s with Su-22s and the older MiG-21s with the MiG-21bis. As it turned out, while MiG-21bis fighters began to arrive in 1979, the Su-22s were initially delayed and only supplied later. In part, this was out of wariness about Amin, but also a lack of trained crews. As of June 1979, for example, while the Afghans had 15 Mi-8 helicopters, of which 13 were serviceable, they only had crews for eight of them.

With the invasion, Moscow was presented with a quandary. On the one hand, it wanted a strong and competent DRA Air Force to support Soviet operations and, in due course, allow Moscow to withdraw its forces. At the same time, it had severe doubts not only about the competence of many Afghan pilots and ground crew, but also their loyalties. While many of its officers had been trained in the Soviet Union, most were affiliated with Amin's radical Khalq faction of the PDPA, not new leader Karmal's more moderate Parcham. On invading, the Soviets grounded the Afghan Air Force until they had had a chance to screen its officers, especially flight crew as there was a fear that they might either wilfully sabotage missions or simply defect to Pakistan. Although Soviet pilots did crew some Afghan aircraft, over time the DRA Air Force did begin to play a greater role. It was never especially well equipped or trusted though, and unlike the army, where some units such as the Commandos did acquire a reputation for competence and discipline, they continued to be treated with suspicion by the 40th Army commanders.

Often, for example, they were assigned secondary and less crucial roles, only briefed about their missions right before take-off, sometimes even while in the air. Soviet 'advisers' were also attached to Afghan Air Force units, as watchdogs as much as allies. They were supplied with some newer equipment, including Su-17 fighter-bombers and Mi-24 gunships, but largely they fielded rather dated airframes, most of which were often unusable because of poor maintenance: Il-18 and Il-28 bombers, MiG-17 and MiG-21 fighters, Su-7 and Su-17 fighter-bombers and Czech-made L-39 trainers.

The dated Ilyushin Il-28 bomber was introduced by the Soviets in 1950. It had already been retired from service, but was still in use by the DRA. (Sovfoto/Universal Images Group via Getty Images)

# DEFENDER'S CAPABILITIES
## Countering Soviet air power

In essence, this would seem a rather one-sided struggle given that the rebels had no air power, but for that very reason, they developed a wide range of responses to degrade Soviet/DRA capabilities, deny them tactical options and minimise their risks. These ranged from how they changed their own modes of operation, such as moving at night and employing camouflage and deception, to how they fought back. In popular mythology, the advent of Western-supplied MANPADS and most notably the Stinger turned the tide of the war, especially in the air. In fact, just as the Soviets quickly developed their own ways of dealing with this threat, so too the *mujahideen* were hardly helpless beforehand.

In part, this was simply a matter of getting used to the new technologies they were facing. In 1978–79 before the invasion, for example, the helicopter was often a startling novelty to government and rebel fighters alike. It reached the point that some DRA infantry units would only advance under fire if they had the totemic support of a helicopter, while likewise it still had the capacity to strike fear into rebel hearts. In one instance, a DRA unit was hard-pressed by *mujahideen* who had ambushed and trapped them in a ravine. They called for air cover, but the only helicopter available was an Mi-24A and this was midday in summer, and the ground temperature was over 50 degrees. From a landing pad 2,000m above sea level, it was questionable whether the gunship could even take off. The crew desperately jettisoned everything they could, including weapons and ammunition, drained the fuel tanks as far as possible and even stripped to shorts and t-shirts. Thanks to a take-off run, they were just able to make it into the air, and when the gunship came into view, the rebels hastily beat a retreat, unaware that there was nothing it could have done to them.

The rebels quickly learnt, though, and became astute connoisseurs of not only the respective strengths and weaknesses of different fixed-wing and rotor threats, but also the tactics the Soviet and DRA pilots would adopt. A British adviser who worked with them in 1987 later reminisced: 'I was taking tea on a mountain-side camp site one morning when we heard the sound of approaching helicopters. I immediately jumped up and began to pack away my stuff to take cover, when I noticed my hosts were still sitting round the pot. One of then laughed and told me to relax, that from the sound of it, it was following the parallel valley, and that it was flying heavy, so it was probably just a resupply run. And he was right.'

## Deception, evasion and camouflage

The *mujahideen* had not had to fear the DRA's poorly motivated and maintained air force, and so had not been used to having to consider the threat from above. They quickly adapted to the new realities after the Soviets arrived, though. In the early stages of the war, the rebels would still often move in larger units numbering in the hundreds. However, they soon came to realize that this made them both more detectable from the air and a much better target. In March 1980, for example, a pair of armed Mi-8 assault helicopters came upon a force of perhaps a hundred rebels assembled outside Chaghcharan, and in just a couple of passes their rockets and outrigger guns had killed or wounded almost half of them. As a result, they took to moving in dispersed groups of 15–20 men, only coming together at the last minute to stage attacks. They also moved at night or towards the end of the day, when a low sun cast long, dark shadows in the rough terrain of the highlands, and weather conditions were typically less conducive to aerial operations. Meanwhile, their bases were hidden inside regular buildings in villages, or in caves, and often camouflaged.

## Anti-aircraft artillery

While for the rebels the best thing was not to be seen, or at least not to be recognized for who they were, this was often not possible. Although nothing could be done against

A perennial problem for Soviet aircrew was the sheer difficulty of spotting and targeting rebels in the rough terrain of Afghanistan, like these rebels manhandling BM-12 rockets to a firing position. (Photo by Robert Nickelsberg/Liaison)

The *Degtyaryova-Shpagina Krupnokaliberny* (DShK) or Degtyaryov-Shpagin Large-Calibre 12.7mm HMG is a design originally dating from 1938, but which continued to prove devastating against low-flying aircraft or thin-skinned or lightly armoured ground targets. (Pascal Manoukian/Sygma/Sygma via Getty Images)

attacks from high altitude, against helicopters and low-flying aircraft, at first they had no real option but to adopt what the Soviets called the 'Chinese method' – essentially, opening up with everything they had, laying down a wall of small-arms fire in front of the target, into which they hoped it would fly. Given the limitations of the rebel arsenal in the early months and years, with 7.62mm AK-47s supplementing vintage .303 Enfield rifles, as well as their lack of formal training, this was extraordinarily ammunition-inefficient and rarely especially effective, even though often they would help scare inexperienced Soviet helicopter pilots into higher altitudes, from which their attacks in turn were less accurate.

Soon, though, they began to acquire 12.7mm DShK HMGs and 14.5mm ZPU anti-air HMGs, either captured from Soviet or government forces or brought over by defecting units of which, especially in the early months, there were many. These had effective firing ranges of 2,000m and 1,400m, respectively, and while heavy and clumsy, began to become common sights defending rebel strongholds. Indeed, in 1984, a batch of 40 20mm Oerlikon autocannon arrived in Afghanistan courtesy of the CIA, a harbinger of the Stingers that would arrive in 1986, as discussed below. Chinese Type 54 HMGs, a licence-built version of the DShK, was also fielded in growing numbers, supplemented by twin-barrel 23mm ZU-23-2 AA gun mounts, which extended the rebels' reach to 2,500m.

Rebel villages and bases were increasingly heavily defended, and the rebels, through both training assistance from abroad and simple combat experience, became more proficient in the use of anti-aircraft fire. Pilots would recall mountainsides 'sparkling' with gunfire, and the rebels would site camouflaged gun positions to support each other. One Mi-8 helicopter pilot recalled a particularly difficult operation in a valley, in which he banked sharply to avoid the fire from one gun position, to find himself literally locking eyes with the crew of another, who had just rolled their DShK out of concealment. 'They looked at me, for a moment, I looked at them, then they started firing and I pulled the throttle right out and climbed for my life.' When he prepared to land back at Bagram, he discovered that his landing gear had been shot away.

The Soviets responded by often adding a pair of aircraft or helicopters to provide air defence suppression support to other missions, typically using rockets to try and neutralize the defences, but this was often of limited value given that the rebels tended to keep their gun positions dispersed and took to having multiple crews available to replace casualties. Furthermore, as the rebels acquired more vehicles, notably Soviet-built GAZ-66 off-road trucks and the iconic Toyota pickups, captured in battle and bought in Pakistan, respectively, it became easier for them to deploy guns in mobile support of their attacks and relocations, too.

## MANPADS

Although Soviet forces involved in the initial invasion had deployed with their full anti-air capacities, just in case the DRA Air Force proved a threat, they quickly returned most dedicated AA units once it was clear this would not be an issue. The only exception was a number of ZSU-23-4 self-propelled anti-air gun systems, which had proven effective as a direct fire support weapon. Nonetheless, some of their 9K32 Strela-2 (Arrow-2, NATO designation SA-7 Grail) shoulder-fired infra-red-homing surface-to-air missiles had already gone missing, and others were in DRA service. No wonder that some of these MANPADS made their way into rebel hands, soon to be supplemented by Chinese HN-5 and Egyptian Sakr Eye versions.

Like the equally dated US FIM-43 Redeye system the CIA then began to supply, the Strela-2 proved something of a disappointment, barely adequate against helicopters and slower transport aircraft, and essentially ineffective against jets. Furthermore, the Soviets quickly adopted countermeasures, from exhaust shrouds to reduce the aircraft's IR signature, to flare dispensers to decoy the missiles away. Many of the missiles, especially those bought

The Strela-2 was a relatively crude MANPADS, but it (and Chinese and Egyptian versions) scored some successes, especially against helicopters. (US DOD)

on the black market, also proved faulty. In 1986, 50 British Blowpipe missiles were sent to the rebels, but this was frankly a system of questionable effectiveness – the British had already withdrawn it from service – not least because it required extensive training to be able to use even then. Nonetheless, there were successes. In July 1984, for example, an Mi-6 heavy lifter was hit by what is thought to have been a Strela-2. The helicopter caught fire and crashed, killing the crew and 26 passengers. As a result, the Mi-6 was henceforth confined to transporting cargo, not soldiers, because of the potential casualties if one was shot down.

In September 1986, though, the rebels started to receive shipments of the much more capable FIM-92 Stinger from the United States, a modern and lethal system. There has inevitably been much debate and dispute about its impact on the battlefield, compounded by the fact that its arrival in numbers essentially coincided with a scaling down of Soviet combat operations, so it is harder to prove that it had quite as dramatic an effect on reducing helicopter and low-level ground attack operations as some claimed at the time. US Representative Charlie Wilson from Texas, one of the driving forces behind Operation Cyclone, the CIA-led programme supplying the *mujahideen* with weapons, claimed – in a striking conflation of American establishment and Afghan rebel interests: 'We never really won a set-piece battle before 26 September' – the presumed date of the first successful use of a Stinger to bring down a Soviet aircraft – 'and then we never lost one afterwards.'

This is demonstrably untrue, in that the Soviet/DRA forces never lost the capacity to project force successfully on the battlefield. After all, as discussed below, the Soviets quickly reacted with a range of new measures, from increased countermeasures on their aircraft to 'Stinger hunts' by *Spetsnaz* commando teams tasked with intercepting inbound shipments. Nonetheless, it is impossible to deny that it did force them also to adapt in ways that often made their air operations less effective. Most notably, strike aircraft were immediately banned from making attacks at altitudes lower than 4,500m, which inevitably took its toll on their accuracy.

The first known successful use of a Stinger in Afghanistan was on 25 or 26 September 1986, when a fighter from the radical Islamist Hezb-i-Islami group shot down an Mi-24 of the 335th OVP near Jalalabad. Over the course of the war, the CIA provided 250–500

## Surviving on the ground

While every effort was made to protect the aircraft, from the armour plating on the Mi-24 and Su-25, to the countermeasures deployed to decoy missiles, it was inevitable that there would be casualties in flight and crashes. There was inevitably a trade-off between protection and convenience, something as true of the experiments with thick bulletproof glass in portholes to the body armour proposed for helicopter crews in 1980. This almost medieval kit comprised a steel breastplate, greaves for the legs and vambraces on the arms. Unsurprisingly, it was immediately rejected as too hot, heavy and cumbersome, although some would use the later BZh-1 set with titanium breastplate and shoulder guards. Instead, helicopter crews and some ground-attack pilots would occasionally wear the 6B2 vest – which was still an ungainly 5kg – not least in winter when it doubled as cold-weather gear, and the ZSh-3B armoured flight helmet. Even their coveralls were changed, first to replace a synthetic that would melt when exposed to fire, and from 1984 they wore camouflage instead of their distinctive light blue.

This last was specifically in case they were shot down and needed concealment. Just as with medical evacuations, Afghanistan saw the Soviets take search and rescue (SAR) much more seriously than in the past. There were SAR helicopter teams on permanent stand-by at Kabul, Bagram, Shindand and Kandahar, and fixed-wing and rotor assets alike would regularly be diverted to try and locate, protect and extract downed airmen. Just in case, flight crews were issued not only survival kits but also PM pistols. These were poorly regarded for their lack of range and authority, though. Many flight crew would replace them with TT Tokarev or APS Stechkin pistols or with Western pistols bought on the black market or looted from dead rebels, with 9mm Beretta 92 and .45 Colt M1911s being especially favoured. Increasingly, they would also acquire the AKS-74U assault carbine version of the standard AK-74 rifle, appreciating its shorter length. Many would also replace one of the water flasks in their survival kit with four RGD-5 hand grenades – it was a common pledge, even if only rarely executed, that the last one would be saved to ensure the airman was not captured by the rebels.

launchers and at least 500 missiles (some claim rather more), and the rebels themselves claimed that with 340 firings they brought down almost 270 aircraft. This is nonsense, as it not only suggests a 79 per cent kill probability – when trained soldiers of the Pakistani military fired 28 missiles, they had no kills – but it is also greater than the total number of Soviet and DRA aircraft downed in the war from September 1986. Official but secret General Staff assessments declassified after the collapse of the USSR suggested a kill probability of just over 10 per cent, which seems more plausible and a perfectly creditable performance in the circumstances.

A cockpit photo of the pilot of a MiG-23 fighter. (Patrick Aventurier/ Gamma-Rapho via Getty Images)

| Main rebel AA weapons | | | | |
|---|---|---|---|---|
| Weapon | Type | Warhead | Range | Notes |
| DShK | 12.7mm HMG | – | 2,000m | Also Chinese Type 54 |
| ZPU | 14.5mm HMG | – | 1,400m | Also on twin ZPU-2 mounts |
| ZU-23-2 | 23mm twin-barrel autocannon | – | 2,500m | |
| Oerlikon KAD | 20mm autocannon | High explosive or armour piercing rounds | 1,500m | 40 supplied |
| Strela-2 | MANPADS | 1.15kg | 3,700m | |
| Redeye | MANPADS | 1.06kg | 4,500m | 50 launchers supplied |
| Blowpipe | MANPADS | 2.2kg | 3,500m | 50 launchers supplied |
| Stinger | MANPADS | 1.02kg | 3,800m | 500 launchers supplied |

# Mines and ambushes

The growing arsenal of guns and missiles at the disposal of the *mujahideen*, combined with their increasing experience, allowed them, in a way, to take the battle to the

# AA Ambush, Panjshir, 1984

The side valleys of the Panjshir were often used as both supply lines and escape routes for rebels during one of the periodic offensives launched by the Soviet/DRA forces. The Soviets would often seek to interdict movements along them, either by airlifted special forces or by helicopters on 'free hunting' missions. Especially by 1983, Massoud's men took advantage of this to stage anti-air ambushes such as this one during the Panjshir VII offensive, the largest undertaken.

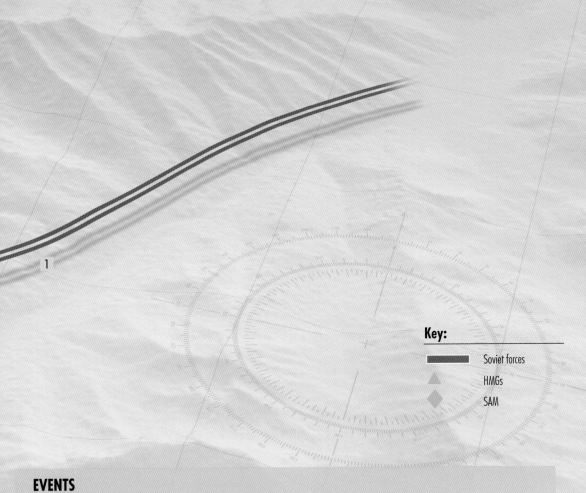

**Key:**

| | |
|---|---|
| ▬▬▬ | Soviet forces |
| ▲ | HMGs |
| ◆ | SAM |

## EVENTS

1. On 28 April 1984, a flight of two Mi-24D gunships noticed a small caravan of half a dozen pack mules heading towards the main valley. This was a decoy, specifically intended to look suspicious, given that most traffic was away from the fighting. In accordance with their usual doctrine, the helicopters approached at high altitude and then dived in low to attack or investigate.

2. As they passed a well-fortified and camouflaged position in a cave in the valley side, a 12.7mm DShK HMG opened up on them, followed by other rebels using small arms, from the valley floor.

3. It seems to have done no damage, but the Soviets quickly gained altitude to move away from the disconcerting amount of fire they were taking.

4. This allowed a team armed with at least two Strela-2 MANPADS to attack them from another hide further along the valley. Given that the missiles' relatively simple IR seeker had great trouble distinguishing a target against the ground, the rebels needed to fire upwards to have any chance to strike. One missile missed, while the other appears to have hit but only lightly damaged its target. Nonetheless, that helicopter left the field of battle, while the second, seemingly intent on revenge, dropped down slightly and swung back around to engage the attackers.

5. In the process, it moved closer to the other wall of the valley, where it was engaged by another hidden DShK. Seemingly deciding that discretion was the better part of valour, the remaining Mi-24 accelerated down the side valley, spraying the floor with its Yak-B machine gun to suppress rebels there, then heading into the main Panjshir Valley.

**OPPOSITE** AIRBASE SECURITY

enemy air forces. With MANPADS, they could target aircraft that usually flew above their operational ranges while they were vulnerable taking off or landing. As a result, transport aircraft took to flying in tight, steep and uncomfortable corkscrews above airfields to try to minimise their exposure, escorted by Mi-24 gunships scattering flares to blind or decoy missiles. This became enough of a constant threat that it even contributed to a powerful scene in the 2005 film *9 Rota* (Ninth Company) in which newly arrived soldiers witness the fiery end of an An-12 hit by a missile right after their landing at Bagram.

Even more sophisticated were the 'air ambushes' that the *mujahideen* would stage, capitalizing on the Soviets' reliance on air power. Tempting targets such as apparent arms caravans would be used to lure helicopters or ground-attack aircraft into tight spaces where they would have trouble responding quickly, when they could be caught in a crossfire of HMGs. In more sophisticated examples of such an ambush, a MANPADS team would be ready for when the Soviets tried to flee the trap, as from behind they provided the ideal target for heat-seeking missiles.

Furthermore, a Soviet dependence on standard operating procedures, as well as often a lack of alternatives, meant that the rebels learned to mine likely helicopter landing sites, whether with regular mines or improvised explosive devices, often – in an ironic touch – made from unexploded bombs. The first Mi-6 heavy transport helicopter lost in action, for example, was in 1981, when landing in the Lashkar Gah area on a regular supply run. As it touched down, it triggered a landmine, probably a Soviet-made TM-57 anti-tank mine with 6.5kg of high explosive. The helicopter was completely destroyed, although the crew were able to scramble free from its burning wreckage.

Ahmad Shah Massoud, commander of the Panjshir Front, communicating with his commanders by field phone. (Photo by Robert Nickelsberg/Getty Images)

## Raids

An even more aggressive approach was to launch pre-emptive attacks on airbases to damage or destroy aircraft before they could be used. Often, this was by long-range fire, using mortars or rockets to bombard the base then retreating quickly before counter-battery fire or a helicopter sortie could be launched in response. The Soviets tried to patrol heights near bases, clear vegetation from potential firing positions to try and make any rebel movement more obvious, and pushed their security cordons wider and wider. Mi-24 gunships were kept in constant readiness, but in practice there was little they could do to lessen this as a constant threat.

More daring yet would be direct assaults on airbases. Each was at the centre of a series of defensive perimeters, whose scale and complexity depended on the size of the base (see figure opposite). To minimise the risk of sabotage, DRA personnel were generally not allowed within the inner perimeter without a special pass, and there would be minefields, watchtowers, guard dog patrols and strongpoints. Each airbase had its own protective detachment drawn from the Separate Guard Battalions (OBO: *Otdelny Batalon Okrany*), which were directly subordinated to the 40th Army command and often supplemented by elements from local Soviet and DRA units.

MINEFIELD

OUTER SECURITY PERIMETER
SOVIET OR DRA SECURITY PERSONNEL

INNER SECURITY PERIMETER
SOVIET SECURITY PERSONNEL

FLARE AND MOTION
SENSORS

| Airbase Separate Guard Battalions | | |
|---|---|---|
| Unit | Base | Deployment/notes |
| 233rd OBO | Kabul | 1985–89 |
| 733rd OBO | Kabul | 1979–89 |
| 1351st OBO | Kabul | 1984–88 |
| 1352nd OBO | Bagram | 1981–89 |
| 1353rd OBO | Jalalabad | 1981–89 |
| 1354th OBO | Kandahar | 1981–89 |
| 1355th OBO | Surubi | 1981–83; then rolled into 1083rd Separate Road Control Battalion |
| 1356th OBO | Shindand | 1981–89 |
| 1357th OBO | Kabul | 1981–88 |
| 1358th OBO | Gazni | 1981–89 |
| 1359th OBO | Kunduz | 1981–83; then rolled into 1083rd Separate Road Control Battalion |
| 1360th OBO | Kunduz | 1984–89 |

Nonetheless, the *mujahideen* continued to raid airbases directly, appreciating the degree to which *Shuravi* air power was crucial to their capacity to launch attacks, guard their convoys and resupply their troops. Ahmad Shah Massoud, the 'Lion of Panjshir', would prove to be a particularly daring master of the raid. During the preparations for the Panjshir V offensive in 1982, he clearly got wind of the Soviets' plans and on 25 April launched an attack on Bagram airbase. His fighters infiltrated the outer perimeter, which in those days was simply a chain-link fence topped with barbed wire, and then opened fired on the aircraft parked on the apron with mortars and rockets. Their claim was that they destroyed 23 aircraft, but while this is an exaggeration – they seem to have destroyed or seriously damaged six, and slightly damaged more – it was undoubtedly a shock to the Soviets at the time.

As a result, the Soviets would make their bases increasingly formidable strongholds over time, with multiple perimeters, sound and motion detectors, dogs and deliberately irregular patrols, and tripwire flares and mines. Nonetheless, the weak point was so often still the human factor. In June 1985, for example, rebels managed to get onto the DRA part of Shindand airbase – as a security measure, the Soviets kept their operations separate – by simply bribing the security detail, and proceeded to damage or destroy a number of Afghan Air Force MiG-21s and Su-17s.

# Pakistan and Iran

Neither Pakistan nor Iran were directly involved in the war, but its fluid nature and their support to different degrees for various rebel factions meant they also played a direct role in the air war. Over the course of the war, millions of refugees crossed the border into Pakistan, and rebels began adopting Pakistani territory for havens to regroup, recover and acquire weapons. This became increasingly institutionalized as Pakistan became used not only by the US for its activities in support of the *mujahideen* but also by China and other donors such as Saudi Arabia. In due course, the Soviets launched cross-border raids on rebel bases, and in other cases pilots accidentally strayed over the frontier. Islamabad claimed that in 1979–85 alone, there were 615 border violations by Afghan and Soviet aircraft. While this may be an exaggeration, it is clear that there was a deliberate willingness to cross into Pakistani airspace, whether in hot pursuit of retreating rebels or, more often, to strike at bases and supply routes. In the main, the Pakistani government did not react directly, not least because its relatively aged Mirage III and Chinese-built MiG-19 aircraft were not generally able to intercept the Soviets in time. There were incidents, though, and once Pakistan had received new F-16 fighters from the US, it felt more comfortable with confrontation. The Soviets began routinely attaching a pair of MiG-23MLD fighters with air-to-air missiles as escorts to flights involved in operations near or over the border. Even so, in August 1988, a Pakistani F-16 shot down an Su-25 piloted by Alexander Rutskoi, a decorated airman who was later made a Hero of the Soviet Union and went on to become a vice-president of Russia, while he was apparently leading an attack on a rebel training base just inside Pakistan. Iran played a much less active role, but in September 1988, two Soviet MiG-23MLs intercepted and downed two Iranian AH-1 SuperCobras that had intruded into Afghan airspace.

# CAMPAIGN OBJECTIVES
## A decade in Afghanistan

The Soviet approach to the war changed over time, and with it the role of its air power. What was originally envisaged as a short-term measure to impose a more moderate and pragmatic leadership under Babrak Karmal and create a breathing space in which to heal the wounds in the PDPA and country caused by Amin's purges, and deal with the still-nascent rebel challenge, increasingly became regarded as a long-term commitment. The PDPA leadership proved unequal to the task, the rebellion grew, foreign assistance augmented the capacities of the *mujahideen*, and while the Soviet leadership kept talking wistfully of plans to withdraw, this looked like a pipedream until a new team under reformist Mikhail Gorbachev was willing to grasp the nettle and acknowledge that this was, in effect, an unwinnable war. Thus, the war could broadly be conceived as having been fought through five broad phases.

The An-22 was a powerful heavy lifter used primarily to transport vehicles and supplies. (Russian MOD)

| Commanders of the Air Force of the 40th Army | |
|---|---|
| Major General Boris Lepayev | 1980–81 |
| Major General Vladimir Shkanakin | 1981–82 |
| Major General Sergei Kalensky | 1982–83 |
| Major General Gennady Kolodiy | 1983–85 |
| Major General Viktor Kot | 1985–86 |
| Major General Dmitry Romanyuk | 1986–89 |

## 1. Invasion, 1979–80

Although official Soviet documents were often shrouded in euphemism and riddled with deliberate omissions – often cryptic and unelaborated references to 'verbal reports' and 'agreed decisions' – it is nonetheless clear how far initially this genuinely was expected to be a brief operation. Directive No. 312/12/001 of 24 December 1979 giving approval to the deployment of Soviet troops, signed by Defence Minister Ustinov and Foreign Minister Gromyko, simply says that: Considering the military-political situation in the Middle East, the latest appeal of the government of Afghanistan has been favourably considered. The decision has been made to introduce several contingents of Soviet troops deployed in southern regions of the country to the territory of the Democratic Republic of Afghanistan in order to give international aid to the friendly Afghan people and also to create favourable conditions to interdict possible anti-Afghan actions from neighbouring countries…

Despite the apparent success of Operations *Storm-333* and *Baikal-79*, already by early 1980, there were signs that the Politburo – in effect the ruling cabinet of the Soviet Communist Party – was beginning to appreciate that this might not be quite as quick and easy as expected. On 7 February 1980, the Politburo convened to hear a report from Yuri Andropov, head of the KGB, who had returned from a trip to Kabul. Defence Minister Ustinov suggested that 'we must speak very carefully regarding a withdrawal of forces from Afghanistan'. In his view, stabilizing Afghanistan would take 'about a year, maybe even a year and a half', and that 'before that, we cannot even think about a withdrawal of troops, otherwise we may incur much unpleasantness'. Soviet leader General Secretary Brezhnev agreed, adding that 'we even need to increase the contingent of forces in Afghanistan somewhat'. Until a decision on that had been made, though, the primary goals of this early stage were marked by a focus on the initial seizure of the country and air missions were largely confined to the ferrying in of the invasion forces and limited security operations.

## 2. Reluctant escalation, 1980–84

Bit by bit, the OKSVA expanded and was adapted to a longer-term deployment, with the withdrawal of essentially redundant elements such as anti-aircraft units and several tank elements. It was not as if there was any great enthusiasm on the Soviet leadership's part for the war, but instead there was a dawning realization of just what a task they had taken on,

The cost of the war was terrible for both humans and infrastructure. Here a victim of the war makes his way past buildings in Kabul, likewise shattered in the fighting. (Peter Turnley/Corbis/VCG via Getty Images)

# A secret war

The Soviets' capacity to learn the lessons of the war were undoubtedly hindered by the fact that, in its early years at least, it was officially not being fought. Only by 1985 was there any real public discussion of the conflict as anything other than limited and sporadic attacks by 'bandits', and those who fell in battle were usually listed as having died in 'training accidents'. This would slowly change over time, not least as more and more veterans returned home – some in zinc boxes – and knowledge of the realities of the situation spread around the country. However, similar secrecy also operated within the military. When Su-24s flew bombing missions in the 1984 Panjshir VII operation, for example, this was recorded in their logs as a 'Combat Training Course' flight. One navigator incautiously recorded a sortie as an actual combat mission, and was reportedly reamed out by the unit's political officer for his temerity.

and a belief that to withdraw would be more dangerous to the DRA and to the USSR's international credibility than escalation.

During his brief tenure as general secretary (November 1982–February 1984), Andropov even explored possibilities for a negotiated withdrawal. He had been originally sceptical about the merits of invasion, and soon appreciated just how dangerous it was for a declining Soviet Union. Nonetheless, this was not a priority for a leader who spent most of his reign in dialysis and was more concerned with trying to line up a coalition of reform-minded younger leaders to succeed him. His half-hearted efforts were in any case quickly derailed by events, including the shooting down of a civilian airliner which had strayed into Soviet airspace in September 1983.

This was therefore a period of gradual and grudging escalation in the scale and tempo of Soviet activity in Afghanistan. The size of the OKSVA would grow from just under 82,000 in 1981 to 93,000 in 1984. New elements more suited to this counter-insurgency were introduced, from additional *Spetsnaz* to sniper teams. Operations ranged from small-scale security missions to major local offensives, but with no clear strategic goals beyond the increasingly illusory notion that the PDPA leadership would be able to reconcile the opposition or that the DRA and Soviet forces could physically eliminate them. As a veteran of the times from the 40th Army command team recalled: 'It was all tactics, no strategy. We were busy as hell, but didn't know what we were actually doing there.'

## 3. Chernenko's war, 1984–86

Andropov died on 9 February 1984, and while he had hoped that his protégé Mikhail Gorbachev would succeed him as general secretary, there was still not enough support for the young reformist. Instead, a pragmatic political deal saw the ageing Konstantin Chernenko elected general secretary with Gorbachev effectively as his deputy and heir. Chernenko was another ailing figure, suffering from emphysema, and this grey and unmemorable figure appears to have fixed on a military victory in Afghanistan as a last chance to make his name for posterity.

He presided over an expansion of the OKSVA and above all a massive and serious escalation of its combat operations, as well as the adoption of more expansive rules of engagement that saw air attacks on population centres used to try and encourage people to flee disputed areas. Although many of the senior commanders on the ground had doubts as to whether this was at all feasible, the Kremlin's commitment – and one held by many of the senior military figures in Moscow – was to force rebel groups either to reach deals with the DRA government or wipe them out.

Chernenko died on 10 March 1985, and while Gorbachev did indeed succeed him, his political position was delicate, as he had only a wafer-thin majority on the Communist Party's

The MiG-23 was designed for a conventional war with NATO but saw its first combat bombing rebel targets in Afghanistan. (Amer Almohibany/AFP via Getty Images)

Central Committee, the wider body that brought together its senior figures and which elected and could remove a general secretary. He considered the war in Afghanistan to be a costly distraction and a mistake, and unlike his predecessors had had no part in the decision to invade, so he could portray it as other people's blunder. As soon as he took power, he began discussions in the Politburo about disengaging from Afghanistan, and they reached a decision in principle on 17 October 1985.

Nonetheless, his difficult political position meant that he had to be careful, and so he allowed the hawks to continue their high-tempo efforts in Afghanistan through that year. In effect, he gave the generals everything they asked for: Gorbachev had to let them fail to win a military victory, before he could make them accept his plan to reach a political settlement.

## 4. The 'bleeding wound', 1986–88

In February 1986, Gorbachev was finally able to make a public announcement of his goal, calling Afghanistan a 'bleeding wound' and expressing the hope that the 40th Army could be withdrawn 'in the nearest future'. Of course, it would not be quite so easy. Moscow needed for both its own security and its global standing to ensure that there was an international deal that would also see the backers of the *mujahideen* end their support for the rebels. The DRA likewise needed to be strengthened so it could survive a Soviet withdrawal, at least long enough not to embarrass the Kremlin.

There were substantial obstacles, from constituencies in the USA and Pakistan who were quite happy to see the war continue to bleed and humiliate Moscow, through to the PDPA leadership itself, which did everything it could covertly to derail the talks, terrified as to what might happen when the Soviets withdrew. In May 1986, Moscow engineered the replacement of Babrak Karmal at the head of the PDPA with Dr Mohammad Najibullah, the head of the KhAD secret police but also a man considered to have the capacity to broker some sort of deal between Kabul and major tribal factions while being tough enough to hold the DRA together. (His GRU dossier said that he was 'vain and ambitious' but also 'an intelligent, clever, and vicious politician'.) Najibullah did institute a new policy of 'national

'Strong be the unshakable Afghan-Soviet friendship' reads the sign between these photos of Soviet General Secretary Mikhail Gorbachev and his PDPA counterpart Babrak Karmal, but, in 1986, Gorbachev would engineer Karmal's ousting in favour of Mohammad Najibullah. (AFP via Getty Images)

reconciliation' with some successes, although he also did what he could to undermine the Soviets' efforts to engineer a withdrawal.[6]

During this period, Soviet combat operations in Afghanistan diminished sharply. Although there were sporadic offensives, usually in response to, or to forestall major rebel attacks, the priority was on maintaining the balance of power on the ground, minimising casualties and building up the strength of the DRA's forces. This was essentially because the debate within Soviet government circles was becoming increasingly pragmatic, as Gorbachev orchestrated a campaign to convince even his more hawkish colleagues that Afghanistan was more trouble than it was worth. Giving a report to a Politburo meeting in November 1986, for example, Chief of the General Staff Sergei Akhromeyev, at Gorbachev's urging, gave his unvarnished perspective: 'After seven years in Afghanistan, there is not one square kilometre left untouched by the boot of a Soviet soldier. But as soon as they leave a place, the enemy returns and restores it all back the way it used to be. We have lost this battle. The majority of the Afghan people support the counter-revolution now. We lost the peasantry, who have not benefited from the revolution at all. 80 per cent of the country is in the hands of the counter-revolution.' Gorbachev followed that up with a stark warning: 'We have been fighting in Afghanistan for six years now. If we don't change our approach, we will be fighting there for 20 or 30 more.'

Meanwhile, talks were under way in Geneva under the auspices of the United Nations, formally between Afghanistan and Pakistan, with the USA and USSR only acting as guarantors, but really as a proxy forum for Moscow and Washington to reach a deal. As a result, no timetable for withdrawal was even drawn up until autumn 1987. By the end of the year, a resolution was essentially agreed, and on 8 February 1988 Gorbachev was able to make a public announcement about withdrawal. The Geneva Accords that provided its basis were signed on 14 April 1988. The OKSVA was going home.

6    As part of this process, the Democratic Republic of Afghanistan was formally renamed the Republic of Afghanistan, but for clarity and convenience, the term DRA will continue to be used.

## 5. Withdrawal, 1988–89

Reaching an agreement on withdrawal was one thing, but accomplishing it in a complex battlespace facing a wide range of often-autonomous rebel forces, many of which had no commitment to the Geneva process, was another. Moscow's aim was to extricate its forces as quickly as possible, but also with the minimum of casualties and in a staged way so as to avoid panic within the government forces or giving the *mujahideen* any momentum.

The field operation was placed in the hands of General Valentin Varennikov, one of the outstanding military planners of his generation, who held the position of Chief Military Adviser in Kabul (and thus virtual military proconsul) and the commander of the 40th Army, Colonel General Boris Gromov, himself a star of the war. The actual withdrawal began on 15 May 1988, and in accordance with Moscow's deal with Washington, would be 'front loaded', with the bulk of the OKSVA withdrawn in the early stage of the operation. Nonetheless, Varennikov and Gromov were determined to make this an orderly process, and they relied on careful coordination, political outreach to the rebels and, where necessary, vivid demonstrations of Soviet firepower.

To this end, the closing phase of the war saw a number of significant operations designed to clear routes for withdrawal and to destroy or deter rebel forces that looked likely to try and capitalize on it. These were essentially successful, and on 15 February 1989, the last Soviet forces rolled back onto Soviet soil over the Friendship Bridge spanning the Amur Darya River that marked the border, Gromov symbolically taking up the rear. The civil war in Afghanistan would continue, and Soviet air power would still play a minor role in the coming months, in support of Najibullah's regime, but in effect, the war was over.

Sporting a banner reading 'Hello Motherland', Soviet paratroopers ride a BTR-60 APC back across the Afghan border to Termez in the USSR on 6 February 1989. (Vitaly Armans/ AFP via Getty Images)

# THE CAMPAIGN
## Jets and helicopters fight a guerrilla war

### 1. Invasion, 1979–80

Even before the invasion, there were Soviet Air Force elements in Afghanistan, with an Mi-24 squadron of the 280th OVP and a squadron of An-12 transports at Bagram airfield, which had become the hub of Moscow's activities there (and where the commandos who carried out *Storm-333* were secretly mustered). As *Baikal-79* began, on 25 December 1979, 55 VTA transport aircraft under Colonel General Ivan Gaydayenko began ferrying troops and vehicles of the 103rd Air Assault Division and additional special forces to Kabul and Bagram. All told, 343 separate flights were made – 200 by An-12s, 77 by Il-76s and 66 by An-22s – which in the first instance would land 7,700 men, 894 vehicles and another 1,062 tonnes of ammunition and stores. The VTA would also suffer its first loss of the war when, nearing Kabul, an Il-76 carrying 37 paratroopers and seven crew lost altitude and crashed into a mountainside. The next morning, weather conditions were too bad to allow a proper search-and-rescue operation, and the Soviets lacked specialists able to manage the terrain. They had to resort to flying in climbers from an army sports club in Central Asia, giving them weapons and five paratroopers as guards, and sending them to scour the area. On 1 January 1980, they finally found the crash site, but everyone on board the aircraft had died on impact.

The bulk of the invasion force was entering the country by land, over the Friendship Bridge and taking the road through Mazar-e-Sharif to Kunduz and then Kabul, or to the west, along the A77 highway to Herat and on to Shindand and eventually Kandahar. Helicopter forces provided cover for these convoys and also deployed units of paratroopers and *Spetsnaz* to take control of key passes and stations along their way. Mi-6s of Colonel Vladimir Bukharin's 280th OVP, for example, landed paratroopers along the highway across the Hindu Kush mountains on the way to Kabul, while Mi-8s deployed from Ashgabat to seize points near the border pass of Kotal-e Rabat-e Mīrza, opening the way for columns moving towards Herat and Shindand.

The medium-range An-12 turboprop transport was a workhorse of the VTA in Afghanistan. (US Navy)

An Mi-8 coming in to land at Kabul airport, with a file of Il-76 transports in the background, 1983. (Francois Lochon/Gamma-Rapho via Getty Images)

# Harbingers of war

With the exception of the bitter fighting associated with *Storm-333* and the seizure of strategic locations in Kabul, the early stage of the operation was pretty bloodless. It would not take long for the backlash to begin, though, with air power having to be unleashed against both rebels and deserting DRA troops. The first combat air sorties took place on 9 January, when a company-sized Soviet convoy on the road to Faizabad was ambushed by a sizeable rebel force, including cavalry. The unprepared mechanized infantry apparently did not cover themselves with glory, staying 'buttoned up' inside their APCs and blazing away through their gun ports to little real effect, but fortunately for them, two pairs of Su-17 fighter-bombers were soon able to engage the attackers with S-5M 55mm rockets, driving them away.

The very next day, in a sign of the nationalist response the Soviet invasion would generate, a mutiny erupted in the DRA's 20th Infantry Division in Baghlan province, and four Soviet MiG-21s flew in support of ground troops sent to crush it. Most operations at first were indeed limited and often small-scale. In the Kandahar area of operation, for example, the only incidents throughout January were a couple of cases of sniping at helicopters lifting off from the airfield, and one sortie to destroy a T-55 tank stolen by defectors from a DRA unit. Perhaps out of boredom, Colonel Bukharin himself took an Mi-24A out to hunt for it, and on locating it, buried it under rubble by dropping a couple of 250kg FAB-250 bombs. Even so, it was a mark of the lack of coordination of those early days, and the assumption that this would not be a serious shooting war, that Bukharin had to spend almost a day getting permission for his flight from Kabul.

Little by little, though, the conflict was escalating, and by the end of January, the 40th Army was issuing new guidelines, allowing local commanders much more of a free hand in deciding when and how to use lethal force. Nonetheless, the close integration of air and ground assets that would be a feature of the later war – which was already evident in some areas – was by no means yet the norm. In March 1980, for example, a substantial operation was launched to restore government control to the Kunar Valley near Jallalabad. Deserters from the DRA's 9th Infantry Division had gone over to the rebels with their guns and a number of BTR-151 APCs and mortars, posing a serious

challenge. The 201ˢᵗ Motor Rifle Division was charged with pushing through the valley and driving out the rebels so DRA security troops could then secure it.

Although the commander of the division had the opportunity to use air assets, he stuck with what he was familiar with: a massive preliminary bombardment by divisional artillery, followed by a mechanized thrust led by tanks. Some rebels fought, most simply melted away. Given that, unlike in later operations, no effort was made to land blocking units by helicopter in side valleys or to use close air support aircraft to prevent the rebels regrouping, this was at best a pyrrhic victory. The rebels were able to return within a few days, and even if the Kunar Valley was a little quieter, this was in many ways a metaphor for so many operations where Soviet mechanized forces tried to engage with the rebels: the latter simply evaded them, and lived to fight another day.

A perennial security challenge was protecting Kabul from rebel night-time attacks, typically by mortar or rocket, launched from the heights around the city, clearly visible here. Regular DRA soldiers, like the one in the foreground, generally proved unwilling to patrol at night, forcing the Soviets to use their own troops or else air power. (Douglas E Curran/AFP via Getty Images)

## Preparing for the air war

As early as the end of February, two more Mi-24 squadrons had been transferred to Afghanistan. At least as important, in a sign of the growing awareness of the degree to which this was going to be a helicopter war, the decision was made that every garrison had to have its own helicopter landing pad, within its security perimeter.

Meanwhile, urgent efforts were being made not only to bring the existing airfields up to necessary standards, extending runways and building new hangars and barracks, but also thoroughly to upgrade the electronic infrastructure. New radars and radio stations were set up. To ensure instrumental navigation, guidance points were deployed at the Kabul airfield, RSBN-4, PRMG-4 and PRMG 5 radio navigation systems were set up to aid navigation, as well as RSP-7 and RSP-10 radar landing systems.

While the fighter pilots struggled to divine how best to use their aircraft, their counterparts in the helicopters reported that this was a time of considerable freedom and opportunity to

A Soviet Mi-24 flies overwatch over Afghan soldiers who, in turn, are guarding a Soviet convoy on the Salang highway, north of Kabul. (Robert Nickelsberg/ Getty Images)

explore what their craft could do without yet much fear of attack from the rebels. In April 1980, Marat Tishchenko, legendary general designer of the Mil Helicopter Design Bureau, visited Afghanistan to see how his airframes were coping and what might be needed to respond to the demands of the environment. He was treated to a demonstration of aerobatic manoeuvres by both Mi-8s and Mi-24s, with corkscrews and barrel rolls that apparently so amazed him that he commented: 'I thought I knew what my helicopters could do, now I'm not so sure.' His main reason to be there was to identify necessary modifications, though, and they were not long in coming. By summer 1980, Mi-24s were being put through field upgrades by Mil technicians which saw new filters fitted to keep sand and dust out of the engines' air intakes and adjustments to the fuel management system to compensate for the high-altitude pressures.

Such measures were reflections of the wider shift to preparing for a long-term counter-insurgency. In June, the Soviets announced a partial drawdown of forces, but this was only half the story. Some units were withdrawn, including the 2K11 Krug (Circle) (NATO: SA-4 Ganef) SAM systems which had accompanied the initial invasion in case the DRA Air Force proved a threat. Furthermore, about 700 of the 1,000 or so tanks which had been part of *Baikal-79* were sent back, having little real value in counter-insurgency. But this was a reorganization rather than a withdrawal, as in their place arrived more paratroopers, *Spetsnaz* and air assets. Moscow was grudgingly coming to realize it was in for a long haul.

## 2. Reluctant escalation, 1980–84

In this stage of the war, the Soviet air campaign was characterized by tactical learning and strategic muddle. The Kremlin may have soon realized this was not going to be a quick and essentially demonstrative operation, but it was uncertain as to quite what it would be instead. There were initial hopes under Andropov that some kind of withdrawal could be negotiated, but little political capital or strategic space for any deal. There was a gradual increase in the size of the OKSVA, but no clear notion as to whether the goal was to try and win a military victory or instead focus on hearts and minds and thus operate largely in support of DRA political and security missions. As a result, the 40th Army's aviators and planners were largely left to their own devices and instead focused on local gains and the process of adapting airframes and tactics developed for very different kinds of war to the Afghan counter-insurgency.

## The continuing rise of rotor power

By the end of 1980, the 40th Army's helicopter force had doubled, bringing it to 251 of various kinds. They were carrying out three-quarters of all close air support missions, and were becoming integrated into all operations, and in particular combined operations. Increasingly, Soviet forces would, in effect, deploy in three: dismounted infantry, their APCs or IFVs consolidated into a *bronegruppa* or 'armour group' as a mobile reserve for attack or transport, and helicopter support. As a former major of the 201st Motor Rifle Division in Kunduz recalled: 'When we first went in, Army Aviation was something handled at the highest levels. Back home, when on exercises, we would have to put in requests to divisional command for support and see what the "gods" decided. Then, when we did get choppers attached to an operation, it was all very by the book – separate chains of command, everything pre-programmed and drawn out on maps with grease pencil, little room for flexibility. That was what the problem in Kunar had been, but it was amazing just how quickly things could change when there are real bullets flying. By 1981, we'd plan missions from scratch together with the "blue-suits", and when everything went wrong, we'd make the next moves up as we went along... We didn't always get things right, for sure, and half the time our after-action reports were wonderful works of fiction, but we were a team.'

Furthermore, Afghanistan was becoming a theatre for the testing of not just new helicopter tactics but also new weapons. The ODAB-500 thermobaric bomb, for example, had never before been used in combat. In August 1980, it was used for the first time against rebels who were well sheltered in caves in the Fayzabad Gorge. Their location meant that regular HE bombs were proving of limited effect, so an Mi-24D was armed with two ODAB-500s, fuel-air munitions which disperse a cloud of volatile ethylene oxide, which is then ignited to cause a massive explosion and pressure wave. Although the bomber had released the bombs from a higher altitude than standard guidance had required, it was nonetheless severely jostled by the blast. The effect on the ground was rather more striking, with all the rebels killed either in the blast or from the rockfall that it produced.

ODABs would continue to be used sporadically through the war, even though they proved temperamental, their effectiveness often compromised by the air temperature (which affected the dispersion of the aerosolized explosive), the height and speed of release and manufacturing issues, so anything between 15 and 50 per cent did not actually work as intended. When they did, though, they were dramatic in their lethality, and thanks to the real-world experience gained by the helicopter crews using them, the guidelines were changed to require that they not be dropped closer than 1,500m to friendly troops.

## Operation *Rhombus* and the Yak-38

The use of Afghanistan as a laboratory and testing ground was not confined to the helicopter fleet and ordnance. If Soviet forces were going to be in Afghanistan a while, it would be important to ensure their fixed-wing aircraft could operate in its conditions, given that they were mainly designed for more temperate climates and conventional wars. To this end, Operation *Rhombus* was a mission staged between April and June 1980, under the direct command of Major General Vladimir Alferov, head of the Air Force's Scientific Research Institute. A special squadron was formed, known as the Rhombus Group, to give

An Afghan worker unloads supplies of flour from the cavernous interior of a Soviet An-22 under the watchful gaze of a Soviet guard at Kabul airport. (Reuters/Richard Ellis)

final approval to the Su-25 ground-attack aircraft and above all to test the performance of the experimental Yak-38 (NATO designation Forger-A) naval vertical take-off and landing (VTOL) fighter.

Rhombus Group comprised two Su-25 and four Yak-38s, as well as some 200 test pilots, engineers and specialist security troops. After it was formed at the Soviet airbase of Akhtubinsk, Rhombus Group was then airlifted to Shindand, an airfield some 1,200m above sea level. While the Su-25s flew there under their own power, the Yak-38s were delivered in An-22 transports. Such was the secrecy of the mission, that the force had their own separate tent city, behind two perimeters, the first maintained by special forces attached to Rhombus Group, and the outer maintained by a motor rifle company.

The Su-25 lived up to expectations and was quickly approved, but the Yak-38 proved much less satisfactory. It was always a clumsy compromise of a design. Given that the Soviet Navy had no large, full-deck aircraft carriers, a VTOL fighter seemed an excellent answer to the constraints of the Kiev-class carriers – technically Heavy Aviation Cruisers in their terms – which could not fly conventional jets. Instead of the vectored thrust nozzles of the British Harrier, the Yak-38 had fully three engines: a main R-28 turbojet for regular flight and two smaller R-38 lift jets in the middle of the fuselage. As a result, it was underpowered and thus unable to carry much of a payload, thirsty, with a maximum combat range of just 195km, and temperamental. If one of the lift jets failed, it would flip over.

In the thin air of the Afghan skies, it fared even less well. It could only fly at dawn or dusk, when the sun had not even further reduced air pressures – but not at night because it lacked that capability. The lift jets scoured the metal and fibreglass landing pad built for them, and whipped up dense clouds of dust that obscured vision and clogged the engine intakes. The naval pilots did make 107 sorties – always accompanied by Su-17s as top cover – but the operation was terminated after a flight accident on 29 May, when a pair of Yak-38s were due to be running strike tests. They were armed with UB-32 57mm rocket pods and meant to test their range when loaded, but first one of the aircraft had to be stood down when its systems failed, and then the second on lift-off suffered a malfunction with one of its lift engines. Its thrust nozzle rotated prematurely into the vertical position and the plane fell back to the landing pad from a height of around 7m. It burst into flames, and although they were soon extinguished, the pilot, Colonel Yuri Kozlov, suffered severe spine injuries. He had to be medevaced first to Kabul and then the Burdenko Central Military Hospital in Moscow.

The aircraft was later repaired, but the limitations of the Yak-38 were clear, even if in fairness it had always been intended as a stop-gap design before the introduction of the supersonic Yak-41M VTOL design (although this would never see service, overtaken by the collapse of the Soviet Union). Nonetheless, Operation *Rhombus* did provide technical data which contributed to the design of the modernized Yak-38M, with proved power plant and air intakes, and optional external fuel tanks to extend its range.

## 'War by plan' in 1981

As the Politburo came to see its involvement in Afghanistan as a long-term commitment, it began to apply the same pernicious (and counter-productive) approaches to the war as it did to the rest of the Soviet system. Above all, this meant the imposition of mechanical and often wildly unrealistic planning targets. At the start of 1981, under pressure from the Kremlin, the Defence Ministry demanded that by year's end, the 40th Army ought 'to liberate at least 70 per cent of the country's territory and 80 per cent of county and local population centres from the rebels'.

It is not as if the military commanders did not realize the foolishness of such metrics. However, this was the will and idiom of the Party and they were forced to work to such targets. For example, one May 1981 report to Defence Minister Ustinov, written by Generals Mayorov, Samoylenko and Cheremnykh, who had all been observing the situation in-country, and counter-signed by Generals Maksimov and Rodin of TurkVO, mixed robust good sense about the failings of the PDPA regime with attempts to illustrate the weakness of these kind of mechanical measures by playing the game: As of 1 August 1980, the DRA government controlled only 134 of 286 provincial districts (46 per cent); as a result of combat operations and work done to organize government rule in the localities, as of 1 May of this year the DRA government controlled 184 of 286 districts (64 per cent), which are practically all of the vital areas of the country. However, as before, rebel influence remains in a majority of the districts which are controlled by the government… Thus, for

## Operation *Rhombus*, 1980

Afghanistan provided an unexpected opportunity to test the Yak-38 naval VTOL aircraft, and here one of the four attached to Operation *Rhombus* is lifting off from its specially made metal launch pad at Shindand airbase, while its Su-17 escort, which has just taken off from the main runway, passes overhead. It is early morning, as the Yak-38 struggles in the thinner air once the fierce Afghan sun has raised the ambient temperature, and the cloud of dust caused by the Yak-38's R-38 lift jets, which would prove a serious problem scouring the aircraft and landing pad alike, is clearly visible. The Yak-38, whose 'bort' or fuselage number 45 shows it is from the Pacific Fleet's 311th Independent Shipboard Attack Air Regiment, is carrying two FAB-250 M-62 bombs for a practice sortie – about the most it was able to carry in Afghanistan, without a rolling take-off. A few months later, this aircraft would be destroyed when its lift engine nozzles failed to rotate during take-off from the Kiev-class carrier *Minsk*. High above, two MiG-21UB fighters from the 27th Fighter Aviation Regiment, heading towards Farah, leave contrails in the morning sky.

A MiG-23 fighter in regular Soviet colours, now on display at the Pima Air & Space Museum in Tucson, Arizona. (Images-USA/Alamy)

the six months (from 1.11.80 to 1.5.81), 63 districts were liberated from the rebels and government rule was established in 31 districts.

The hope seemed to be that this would get Moscow off the OKSVA's back, but the bureaucrats auditing the military's performance within the Central Committee apparatus apparently continued to demand regular reports on progress towards achieving these arbitrary and meaningless quotas at least through to 1983–94. What this did was, in effect, exacerbate an existing Soviet over-concentration on the cities as well as reward questionable over-reporting of positive results. Areas through which Soviet forces swept, like the Kunar Valley in 1980, were dutifully recorded as 'liberated', even if the *mujahideen* returned quickly after they left. Likewise, in many regions the rebels had understandings with local DRA security forces, whereby the government troops would not be attacked so long as they pretended not to notice insurgent activity. Again, though, these areas would duly be registered as government-controlled.

The effects on the air campaign were to harness it to a series of ultimately futile operations that nonetheless allowed the 40th Army commanders to claim progress: mass sweeps of areas that, because there were neither reliable DRA security forces to then hold 'liberated' areas nor adequate hearts-and-minds measures to win over the rural population, soon returned to the *mujahideen*. At the time, there was some serious and often bitter wrangling in Kabul about this. Major General Vladimir Shkanakin, head of the 40th Army's air forces, was apparently sympathetic to the notion that this made no sense but was himself under orders from above to keep his opinions to himself. One officer working in the 40th Army HQ at the time reported a stand-up row between Shkanakin and two colonels in charge of fighter-bomber regiments who had proposed alternative strategies, so the general eventually told his aides that no unit commanders were to get to see him until they had submitted a memo detailing just what they intended to discuss. This rather counterproductive decree was rescinded after a week or so, but it emphasizes not only the degree to which the commanders on the ground had a clear sense that the strategy they

were being forced to apply was not going to be effective – but also how far tight political control of the military prevented, at this time at least, their insights being acted upon, or even reported to Moscow.

Like many later Soviet designs, the T-22M saw its combat debut over Afghanistan, flying long-range bombing missions from bases in the USSR. Its speed, range and capacity to carry 24 tonnes of ordnance made it a threat, even if it relied on targeting data that was often inaccurate or out of date. (Wojtek Laski/ Getty Images)

## Economic war

The only advantage of the Party leadership's increased interference in the war was a new emphasis on addressing its economics. Largely, this meant efforts to deploy more aid in order to shore up support in the towns, as well as development projects (which became magnets for rebel sabotage) which could also foster the expansion of an urban working class, a key component of the PDPA's support. However, it also meant stepped-up efforts to deny the rebels' sources of funding and support. In particular, the KGB tried to undermine support for the *mujahideen* in the West and targeted donors and the intermediaries who converted funds into weapons. However, there was also a role for air power in this campaign.

Ahmad Shah Massoud, the able and charismatic commander of the rebels of the Panjshir Valley, was the beneficiary of gem mines in its upper reaches, especially the lapis lazuli mines of the Jarma region. These were extracted, cut, and then sold across the border in Pakistan, and Massoud taxed the trade for funds. The mines were deep in rebel-held territory, beyond the reach of any but the most extensive ground operation, and well defended. Initially, armed Mi-8s from the Soviet Border Troops contingent were dispatched to raid the mines, but the 'eights' came under an unexpectedly heavy hail of AA fire, forcing them to turn back, damaged. The next plan was to send a full squadron of Mi-24s from Faizabad, but this was ultimately deemed too risky.

Sending FA aircraft was considered next, but also discarded. The range would be extreme, the rather rudimentary navigation and targeting systems on the Su-17 and MiG-21 would have trouble locating the targets amid the gullies and glaciers, and the light bomb loads they could carry would be unlikely to have enough of an impact. As if that were not enough, the mountains tended to generate high winds, and as the mines themselves were some 6,500m above sea level, there was no avoiding this. In 1980, a flight of MiG-21s from the 115th IAP, staging out of Chirchik, had been in the area when it was forced almost 100km from its intended flight path. The fighters barely had the fuel left to make it back to Bagram.

As a result, the decision was made to unleash the Long-Range Aviation. On 10 June 1981, a squadron of heavy bombers flying at 10,000–12,000m dropped more than 400 FAB-500 M-54 high-drag bombs in the area of the mines. Efforts to assess the impact and accuracy of the raid were largely in vain, given the remoteness and the relief of the target. However, while some rebels later responded with bravado, thanking the Soviets for cracking open more seams (as the gemstone was often mined explosively), intelligence reports from the Pakistani markets where they were sold suggested that at least for a couple of years, the supply was distinctly limited.

## The war of the roads

The other side of the coin was to maintain not just the economy of government-held territories, which often came to depend on Soviet food and aid, but also that of the 40th Army. However valuable airlift capabilities were in extreme situations, the overwhelming bulk of men and supplies were moved around Afghanistan by road. The network itself was under-developed, with just 17,000km of roads all told, of which only 2,500km were properly surfaced and could be considered all-season. The main highways ran in a broad U shape from Herat in the west, south to Kandahar, and then bending northwards to Kabul and thence via the strategically vital Salang Tunnel through the Hindu Kush mountains, eventually to Mazar-e-Sharif.

The road network, being crucial to the war effort, inevitably also became a battlefield, with the rebels not only mining it regularly, but also launching ambushes, taking full advantage of the rugged mountains, through which so many of them had to wind. Losses were significant to the convoys and the stress experienced by the crews and escorts on these journeys was, according to participants, rather worse than being in direct combat. Soviet

The rugged Afghan relief is evident from this view of a tunnel road in the north of the country, which also highlights how propitious it was for rebel ambushes of Soviet supply convoys. No wonder their drivers received pennants 'For Valour and Courage' for even as few as 20 successful round trips. (Afghanistan Archive/ Alamy).

supply truck drivers took to painting symbols on their cab doors to show how many runs they had made.

While convoys would be accompanied by advance scout elements, security details in APCs and ZIL-135 gun trucks mounting ZSU-23-2 AA mounts, which were able to rake the hilltops and valley sides, this would nonetheless become one of the most stressful and dangerous, if also unglamorous duties of the entire conflict. Air cover also became a crucial part of the 'war of the roads'. Mi-8s would sometimes be used to land scouts at high vantage points to watch over main routes, but above all, Mi-24 gunships would be detailed to provide top cover for the convoys. Working in shifts, not least because of the need to maintain constant attention, as well as the fuel-inefficiency of keeping pace with the trucks, one or more pairs of Mi-24s would typically monitor the area 2–3km to each side of the route, as well as up to 5km ahead. When ambushes were detected, the gunships would typically engage with guns and lighter S-5 rockets. These were generally regarded as unsatisfactory by the airmen, who preferred heavier ordnance that had a wider blast radius, but not only did the Soviet military have huge stocks of the S-5 they were happy to see run down, but they were also less likely to cause serious damage to the road or trigger landslides.

Given that the convoys often travelled at speeds of 15–20km/h, given the quality of the roads and the need to monitor for mines and IEDs, there was a need for regular refuelling and shift changes, and this prompted the construction of a series of encampments along the routes. The stretch from Termez on the Soviet border to the Salang Pass was generally secured by Mi-24s from Kunduz, for example, with staging stations in Hairatan, Mazar-e-Sharif, Tashkurgan and Pul-i-Khumri. Then they were handed over to gunships based at Bagram, with stations at Jalalabad and Ghazni.

## The Panjshir and Soviet air–land battle

If the 40th Army was to be able to report progress in 'liberating' Afghanistan to the Politburo, it was clear it would need dramatically to improve the coordination of its ground and air elements. As 40th Army air forces commander Major General Kalensky said: 'At present we

Paratroopers from the 5th Company of the 350th Airborne Regiment disembark from an Mi-8 helicopter which is hovering just above the ground to allow for a quick departure. (Sergey Novikov)

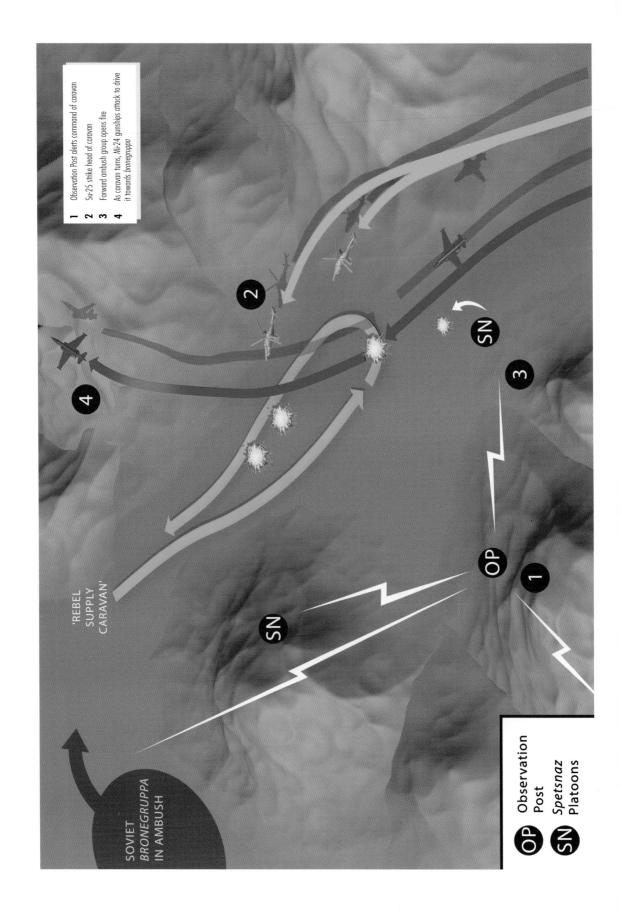

1 Observation Post alerts command of caravan
2 Su-25 strike head of caravan
3 Forward ambush group opens fire
4 As caravan turns, Mi-24 gunships attack to drive
  it towards *bronegruppa*

'REBEL
SUPPLY
CARAVAN'

SOVIET
*BRONEGRUPPA*
IN AMBUSH

**OP** Observation
Post

**SN** *Spetsnaz*
Platoons

**OPPOSITE** CARAVAN INTERDICTION OPERATION

have two armies, one on the ground, and one in the air. We need to bring them together.'
Two particular operations would both track and drive this learning process for the Soviets:
the successive operations launched in the Panjshir Valley – Panjshir V in May 1982 and the
follow-on Panjshir VI in August and September.

Panjshir V reflected both the strengths and weaknesses of the Soviet war. On the one
hand, it was the largest offensive yet against the Panjshir Front. On the other, the objectives
and timing of the operation reflected not so much the needs of the conflict as political
interference. Pressure from Kabul on the Politburo, passed on to the OKSVA, meant that
Lieutenant General Viktor Yermakov, who had only just been appointed latest commander
of the 40th Army, was forced to implement a plan he had inherited from his predecessor,
Lieutenant General Tkach, who himself had believed it was poorly timed and badly
conceived. However, Kabul was desperate to claim that it had finally restored its authority
over the valley, and the Politburo felt it had to accede to its demands for a new offensive.

Some 12,000 Soviet and DRA troops rolled into the valley, hoping not simply to secure
temporary control but also establish bases there. This involved unprecedented coordination
between ground and air forces. Despite Massoud's audacious raid on Bagram, 104 helicopters
and 26 fixed-wing aircraft were directly committed to the operation. Helicopters lifted scouts
ahead of the main attack, and blocking forces both higher up the valley and to commanding
locations overlooking potential rebel escape routes. Right before the main attack, early in
the morning of 17 May, strikes were launched along the whole length of the valley. This saw
the first substantive use of Su-25s from the 200th OShAE, along with MiG-21s and Su-17s.
Su-24 bombers from the 149th Guards BAP based inside the USSR also conducted high-level
bombing runs on villages believed to be rebel strongholds.

The casualties were limited – by now, fighters and civilians alike were used to retreating
to caves and shelters at the first sign of Soviet bombers. However, the point was to damage
defensive infrastructure and disrupt the *mujahideen*, and this was fairly successful, especially
as a preamble to the artillery barrages which followed. Along the sheer mass of forces
deployed, this allowed the Soviet/DRA force to push its way through the valley, albeit not
without setbacks and delays. Mi-24s were widely used for fire support, for the first time using
the new laser-guided 9K114 *Shturm* (Assault) (NATO: AT-6 Spiral) ATGM in numbers. All
told, 559 of these missiles were launched in the course of the operation, at ranges of up to
1,000m, and with levels of accuracy wholly beyond those of earlier wire-guided weapons.

The use of heliborne forces was also not without its problems, especially highlighting the
limited training and experience of many Soviet troops in such operations. Although in total
4,200 troops would be deployed by rotor, with some notable successes, commanders also
reported that many units were still unprepared as to how to conduct themselves in a tactical

# Helicopter assault, 1985

Many Soviet analysts of the war agreed with Major General Grekov, former 40th Army Chief of Staff, that perhaps the single major lesson of the war was the conduct of the heliborne assault. These ranged from large-scale lifts of whole companies or battalions, through to smaller drops of forces intended to observe potential supply routes, block mountain passages or direct fire against the rebels from commanding heights. Here, a Mil Mi-8MT from the 339th Separate Helicopter Regiment drops a squad of paratroopers – whose relative *esprit de corps* and tougher physical conditioning meant they were used disproportionately on such missions – onto a hilltop near the village of Daman, on the Kabul–Kandahar road, during an operation to displace rebels who were using single 122mm rockets, fired from improvised launch rails, to attack supply convoys on the road. The helicopter is hovering just above the ground, a difficult manoeuvre but one which Soviet pilots quickly learnt as a way to ensure they could lift away quickly, its rotors kicking up a cloud of choking dust. Meanwhile, one of the two Mi-24D gunships assigned to support the landing is suppressing the rebel positions with its quad-barrel Yak-B 12.7mm machine gun.

airlift. The most striking use of this capacity was in using Mi-6 heavy transport helicopters to lift 600 soldiers from the 860th Independent Motor Rifle Regiment and the DRA's 20th Regiment to the eastern exit from the valley, relieving a beleaguered Afghan garrison at Dasht-e-Rawat and blocking what had been anticipated would be Massoud's most likely escape route had he chosen to withdraw, as well as a key rebel resupply route from Pakistan.

Like so many such set-piece offensives, Panjshir V was a tactical success yet a strategic failure. After two weeks, and heavy losses, the Soviets had fought their way through the valley. They had proven that the 'Lion of Panjshir' could be beaten, and delivered a serious blow to his forces. Kabul could claim victory in the moment, but within weeks the rebels would be back in the valley, and the government bases and observation points left behind would begin to come under attack.

Hence Panjshir VI, just a few months later, a comparably sized operation that proceeded along broadly similar lines. Envisaged as an attempt to mop up the still-weakened Panjshir Front *mujahideen*, it was really also a desperate attempt to secure government positions before the onset of winter made campaigning that much harder. Again, helicopters were used to deploy blocking forces, largely drawn from the VDV paratroopers and *Spetsnaz*, as well as fire support. This time, though, the preparatory bombardment also saw Tu-16 heavy bombers operating out of Termez inside the USSR targeting rebel villages. Much ordnance was dropped, but to little more avail.

## Lessons learnt

The operation was over – and, needless to say, declared a victory on 10 September, with little real progress made in securing the valley, and the Soviets would be back soon enough. However, these two offensives had also proved extremely important in pinpointing three key issues the 40th Army would have to address in its use of air power. First of all, how to ensure that its bombing missions, while dropping impressive amounts of ordnance, actually hit targets worth hitting. This would put a greater premium on proper prior reconnaissance and also accuracy.

By the end of 1981, before the wider use of the Su-25 gave the Soviets greater tactical flexibility, the Su-17 pilots who carried out the bulk of close air support operations had developed whole new approaches. To suppress rebel air defences before a major strike, for example, a wing of two to four pairs of Su-17s would be deployed. The first pair would be tasked with identifying enemy gun positions from an altitude of 800–1,000m and then marking them with smoke or illumination bombs. Then the remaining aircraft would attack, diving from 2,000–2,500m up and launching 55mm S-5 and 80mm S-8 rockets and RBK-250 and RBK-500 cluster bombs. The aim was to minimize the interval between strikes to prevent the *mujahideen* from reacting, so the suppression run was meant to be within one to two minutes of the designation, and then within another one to two minutes, the main strike group ought to be making its attack. This would typically involve another two to four pairs of Su-17s using S-8 and heavy 240mm S-24 rockets, as well as more cluster munitions and FAB-250 and FAB-500 bombs. Usually, the strike group would make a second run and expend their remaining weapons, before a pair of reconnaissance aircraft would make a pass to assess the impact of the raid.

Secondly, ground, helicopter and fixed-wing operations must be coordinated more closely and smoothly. Commanders complained that, in order to maintain deconfliction, there could be a gap of ten minutes to half an hour between helicopter, artillery and air strikes, allowing the rebels time to reposition and take shelter. One response was the increasing practice of attaching FA and Army Aviation officers to ground units to act as forward air controllers. In keeping with the mass, top-down nature of Soviet doctrine, this had in the past really only been a practice at divisional level, but in Afghanistan regiments and even battalions might have such a 'blue-suiter' attached to them, either long term (this was largely only for VDV and similar elite units) or at least for the duration of an operation.

Thirdly, the deployment of forces by helicopter, even under fire, was clearly a powerful tactical option, but troops – both Soviet and DRA – needed to be better trained to avoid the usual spectacle of their milling uncertainly about immediately after being delivered, often giving the rebels the chance to pick off their officers with sniper fire. In August 1981, for example, a reinforced battalion from the DRA's 20th Division was inserted by air onto a plateau behind the village of Marmoul in the gorge of the same name, part of an operation to relieve pressure on the nearby city of Mazar-e-Sharif. However, because of early losses during landing, they were never able to fight their way down into the valley, and ultimately had to be airlifted out after several days of inconclusive fighting.

This also meant proper support for these helicopter insertions, especially in mountain terrain. Increasingly, they would be carried out by mixed forces of transports and gunships. The Mi-24s would lead the way, typically with one pair on each side of the valley, using guns and rockets to suppress potential ambush points along the route and clear the landing site. Then, as the Mi-8s and Mi-6s began to drop off their charges, the former often not even landing but hovering close to the ground to allow for a quick 'dust-off,' the Mi-24s would circle at an altitude of 1,200–1,800m, ready to respond to any attack.

## 3. Chernenko's war, 1984–86

The previous phase had been one in which Moscow was unwilling truly to come to terms with the scale and nature of the war it had begun. The Politburo tried to run it by plans and quotas, the way it (mis)managed every other aspect of Soviet life. The soldiers of the 40th Army adapted as far as they could, trying to do their best in the circumstances, but lacking any grand strategy that was meant to bring the war to a close. Time and again, generals would hammer home in their reports to Moscow the political dimension, the need for the PDPA seriously to find ways of winning over the mass, rural population, the harm being done by faction-fighting and corruption within the PDPA, but to no avail. There was an abiding suspicion that Karmal and the rest of the DRA leadership were quite comfortable letting the 40th Army do the lion's share of the fighting, while they lived off Soviet assistance. Everything would change, though, when Konstantin Chernenko became general secretary in Moscow. From holding the line while the PDPA – in theory – won over the populace, the 40th Army's mission would, however implausible this really was, actually win this war on the battlefield.

## Genocide from the air?

This changed the tempo and scale of air operations, moving beyond fire support for limited ground attacks and protecting troop and supply convoys, with an increased use of heavy bombing to clear contested areas and punish areas supporting rebels. The US government accused the Soviets of practising 'migratory genocide' by air, especially trying to empty whole regions and force villagers to flee to Pakistan. It is undoubted that there were often brutal operations against civilian targets, especially during this phase of the war, and also the clearing of villages in some sectors, especially when they overlooked strategic locations or were close to main supply routes. However, a comprehensive search of Soviet records of the war during the brief period in which they were opened in the early 1990s found no evidence of any such specific and deliberate approach. Instead, this was probably to mistake the consequences of decisions made on purely military grounds for evidence of some wider policy.

There is no doubt that throughout the war, the Soviets used their air power in an often indiscriminate way, and the direct civilian casualties and indirect consequences, from homes

# Combined air and ground assault, Lashkar Gah, 1985

Lashkar Gah, the capital of Helmand Province, was and still is an important communications hub. Its proximity to the conjunction of the Arghandab and Helmand rivers means it is near one of the cultivated regions the Soviets called 'greens' – because of their vegetation and also the density of rebels typically present in their scattered villages. In May 1985, the Soviets launched a short, sharp three-day operation to suppress rebels who periodically fired mortar and rocket rounds into Lashkar Gah and mounted raids against supply convoys on the nearby roads.

Aqaian Kalay

**Key:**

| | |
|---|---|
| ▬▬▬ | Soviet bombers |
| ▬▬▬ | Soviet helicopters |
| ▬▬▬ | Soviet ground forces |

## EVENTS

**1.** At dawn on the first day, Su-24 bombers from Khanabad staged a medium-altitude bombing raid concentrating on Aqaian Kalay, considered the command centre of the local rebels.

**2.** A Soviet mechanized force supported by DRA Sarandoy security troops out of Lashkar Gah began an encirclement.

**3.** Another mechanized force approached along the river valley from the west.

**4.** Meanwhile, elements of the 22nd *Spetsnaz* Brigade's 370th Detachment were airlifted from Lashkar Gah to several strategic locations both to prevent ambushes and to stop rebels from fleeing

along the cultivated river banks (it was thought less problematic if they headed into open, arid lands where they could be more easily located and neutralized later).

**5.** The next morning, the Mi-24s of the 205th Independent Helicopter Squadron began providing fire support for the ground forces as they continued to advance from the west and the north-east.

**6.** In the main, the rebels simply avoided contact, but in the one serious engagement late on the second day, when they tried to protect a cache of rockets, Su-25s from Kandahar flew low-level bomb and rocket runs to devastating effect.

The Su-17 was a capable fighter-bomber which, as is clear from this photo of the Su-20 export version displayed in Cairo, could carry a wide range of stores. These included, as here, drop tanks with extra fuel to extend their range, rocket pods and bombs. They could also be armed with air-to-air and air-to-surface missiles, and were fitted with two internally mounted 30mm cannon. (LeCaire)

destroyed to means of livelihood ruined, cannot be understated. At the same time, though, rumour and propaganda also ran wild, with all kinds of ultimately disproven claims. One, for example, was that Soviet aircraft were dispersing chemical weapons in a so-called 'yellow rain', although the scientific consensus now is that this was actually, of all things, the result of large swarms of bees defecating digested pollen grains. Even more extreme were the claims that the Soviets air-dropped mines deliberately made to look like toys to attract children: 'Soviet Toys of Death' ran a lurid headline in the *New York Times*. This was based on the PFM-1 mine, bright green and shaped like a sycamore seed, which may have caught children's eyes but were certainly not intended for that.

None of this is to minimize what the Soviets did do, especially during this period. One severely traumatized Su-17 pilot admitted he still had nightmares, four years on, about bombing villages suspected of harbouring rebels. He added that while in 1984, they would often buzz the village first to try and get people to flee, and sometimes helicopters would even drop warning leaflets in advance, by mid-1985, such practices had been officially abandoned. 'We carried out our combat orders, and were not meant to think about the human costs.' Such were the realities of 'Chernenko's war'.

## Panjshir VII: The start of 'Chernenko's war'

The first real expression of this was the Panjshir VII offensive. It had been planned before Chernenko's ascent, but in multiple versions, from an essentially token flag-flying mission in this eternally contested valley, all the way up to a massive operation, the biggest yet. Chernenko, needless to say, went for the maximalist option.

There had been a formal truce between Massoud and the Soviets until autumn 1983, and then a rough-and-ready ceasefire had continued, but the government in Kabul still sought control over the valley, and wanted the Soviets to provide it. They needled the rebels – who, in fairness, were themselves starting to become more aggressive again – and used the resulting clashes to lobby Moscow for a new offensive. In March 1984, they claimed Massoud had refused further peace talks, and Chernenko was happy to use this as an excuse to unleash Panjshir VII.

This would see 15,000 Soviet and DRA troops deployed in April–May 1984, backed by a massive force of 194 aircraft from both within the country and bases in the USSR, and 154 helicopters. The operation was broadly similar to previous ones, but on a different scale and level of intensity. The preliminary bombardments were conducted by squadrons from fully four heavy bomber regiments flying from Soviet bases, as well as the first major operational use of Su-24 bombers from 149th Guards BAP and 143rd BAP. Reconnaissance missions had been flown since the start of April by MiG-21UMs, sometimes dipping down to dangerously low altitudes of 20–30m, relying on high speeds thanks to their afterburners to evade any AA fire. They were supplemented by Su-17MZRs from the 263rd Reconnaissance Squadron and an An-30 photographic platform. Although the high-altitude bombing raids would still hit pre-planned targets, the intention was that this time they would have more accurate and up-to-date coordinates than in the past.

A squadron of Tu-16s from the 200th Guards TBAP made the first pass over the valley, followed by Tu-22M2s from the 1225th TBAP, bombing from altitudes of 9,000–10,000m. Half an hour later, 60 Su-24s criss-crossed the Panjshir at altitudes of 5,000m. Such was the density of aircraft in the sky that special protocols had to be instituted to ensure they kept apart and an An-26RT communications relay aircraft flew in a holding pattern near the valley, to coordinate radio traffic back to the operation HQ.

This first joint raid lasted two hours, and the effect was apparently impressive. In particular, the 64 OFAB-250-270 high explosive fragmentation bombs each Tu-22M2 dropped seemed to churn up a rolling, roiling carpet of explosions. Preparatory strikes lasted for three days, although the heavy bombers would only mount one sortie each day, in the early morning, not least because afterwards the targets were shrouded in dust. The Su-24s were more active, though, including some night-time raids, while hunting pairs of Su-25s would fly through the day. After each bombing raid, the artillery would continue the battering of the Panjshir.

A MiG-21bis, an evolution of the MiG-21 that was pressed into service in Afghanistan as a fighter-bomber. Although hardly optimised for this role, it did have an internal gun and could be fitted with an extra, external fuel tank, as well as two small bombs. (Alan Wilson)

The Soviets – and, to a lesser degree, the DRA forces – established a network of observation posts on commanding heights, which often had to be supplied by air and often supported by air, too, when under attack. Here, a Soviet Mi-24 helicopter passes such a post in May 1988. (Douglas E. Curran/AFP via Getty Images)

Although there is some dispute over this, the consensus seems to be that the actual impact of the high-altitude heavy bombing was less than had been hoped. As already mentioned, the inhabitants of the valley were by now used to bombing raids. Villages and *mujahideen* encampments alike had their hides and bunkers, and even small children knew what to do when they heard the tell-tale sound of jets or helicopters in the sky. The bombs used, most of which were scarcely changed since World War II days, were often under-powered for the task, and many of the bomber crews were more interested in emptying their bomb bays quickly and returning home than concentrating on accuracy. Nonetheless, they did send everyone scurrying to ground, which allowed the insertion of observation and blocking units by helicopter to go relatively unopposed. By the third morning, though, the Su-24s were using a mix of larger FAB-1500 high-explosives and RBK-500 cluster bombs. The former would hit first, shattering buildings and flattening walls, and then the cluster bombs would scatter smaller submunitions that would themselves send hundreds of thousands of 5.5mm steel balls scything across the area, killing any who had been inside or under soft cover.

The offensive was marked by some tough fighting, as well as the continued high tempo of air operations, especially after this initial stage by helicopters and Su-25s (in June 1984, Marshal Sokolov would give the *Grach* his seal of approval, saying 'the Su-25 ground attack aircraft have displayed their good combat capabilities'). Yet even with especially liberal use of air-dropped PFM-1 anti-personnel mines, largely scattered from helicopters, it was never possible reliably to prevent the rebels from disengaging when they chose, and for all the sound and fury – and some thousand Soviet and DRA casualties – the offensive itself, much like the initial high-altitude raids, were impressive to the eye but strategically meaningless. After Panjshir VII, one *Spetsnaz* captain, who had been tasked with assessing the impact of the bombing on the up-valley village of Khenj, openly wondered: 'How many millions of rubles did we just waste blowing up empty houses, and what could we have done in Afghanistan, if we had spent them on new houses?'

# Eagle's nests

It soon became clear to the Soviets that satellite reconnaissance and high-altitude photography were not especially effective in monitoring the movements of rebels and their caravans, picking their way through narrow mountain passes and across rough terrain. In order to try to reduce their strategic mobility and gain early warning of attacks, they soon began to establish numerous observation posts on commanding heights. Some were essentially company firebases, but others were smaller posts manned often by no more than a platoon, known as *Orlinye Gnyozda*, or 'eagle's nests'. Many of these could only practically be reached by air, and Mi-8s were regularly employed rotating garrisons, delivering supplies and evacuating the wounded. In some cases, the posts were so constrained that the helicopters could not even land, either hovering as low as they could (often a hazardous and difficult piloting task in the windy mountain ranges) or at best planting just their nose wheels for stability.

## Operation *Trap*: The end of 'Chernenko's war'

Chernenko had been replaced by Mikhail Gorbachev in March 1985, but he inherited a Central Committee still packed with hard-liners and old-style conservatives, and Marshal Sergei Sokolov as defence minister, a man who had had a key role in running the war in Afghanistan and thus a stake in not admitting it was unwinnable. Lieutenant General Igor Rodionov, who commanded the 40th Army between April 1985 and April 1986, was thus in an awkward position. He himself was sceptical about whether the war could be won, not least as he was scathing about the PDPA, and knew that Gorbachev was no more convinced. Yet Sokolov expected him to try to achieve a military victory, and the Politburo in the first year of Gorbachev's general secretaryship was happy to let the supporters of 'Chernenko's war' undermine their own case.

Rodionov's successor, Lieutenant General Viktor Dubynin, was in a rather happier position, as the Chief of the General Staff, General Akhromeyev, had privately briefed him that the policy was likely soon to change. Initially, Dubynin had therefore on the one hand carte blanche to launch major operations, but on the other a degree of freedom from the Politburo as to what goals to set. He combined the two in Operation *Trap*, launched in August 1986, a combined arms operation intended to eliminate the forces of Ismail Khan,

The Su-25 was one of the most effective combat aircraft of the war, a rugged ground-attack plane with an internal 30mm cannon and, as shown, 11 hardpoints able to carry 4,400kg of stores. (Fedor Leukhin)

a prominent field commander in the Herat region and the rebel stronghold of Kokari-Sharshari, close to the Iranian border.

What was noteworthy about Operation *Trap* was that it demonstrated just how far Soviet capabilities to combine air and ground operations had come, and just what they could do. It was unusual by the standards of the Afghan war in being carried out simultaneously in three separate albeit linked theatres: Herat itself; the wide plains and foothills close to the city; and the mountains of the Sharshari border regions, some 150km away.

Rebel forces were extremely active inside the city and region of Herat. Although periodic security sweeps were launched against them, they could replenish themselves with recruits and supplies from across the region, including the Harirud Valley. This led towards Iran, and which was used for supply caravans. However, it was hard for them to maintain secure arsenals, supply bases and havens for medical recuperation and training close to Herat, even in the so-called 'green zones', densely vegetated regions of shrubs and orchards the rebels used for cover. For that, they had their base at Kokari-Sharshari, which was the stronghold of the rebel field commander known as Ismail Khan, a hard-nosed and competent former officer of the DAR's 17th Infantry Division. The Soviets' aim was thus first to clear the plains around Herat to isolate the urban guerrillas from their lines of supply, then to destroy the Kokari-Sharshari base, and finally to root out the rebel presence in the city of Herat itself.

The ZPU 14.5mm AA HMG was bulky and unsophisticated, but much of the time the best the rebels had at their disposal to guard their bases. (Zubair Mir/AFP via Getty Images)

The operation involved a force of 28 battalions – ten Soviet and 18 Afghan – under 40th Army Deputy Commander Major General Georgy Kondratiev and the air forces were involved at every stage of the operation. First of all, detailed aerial reconnaissance of likely routes of attack and withdrawal was combined with an extensive campaign to sow the trails and fords along the Iranian border with anti-personnel mines dropped from KMGU submunitions

## Operation *Manoeuvre* and the trouble with maps

A recurring problem for the Soviets was that of operating in rough, monotonous terrain where it was difficult for them to orient themselves. Their own GLONASS equivalent of the West's GPS satellite-based navigation system was not in general use, and most air operations were wholly dependent on maps and, where possible, pre-emplaced navigation guidance beacons or simply flares or smoke. This led to a number of unfortunate and even lethal errors, from friendly fire to forces being landed in the wrong place. During Operation *Manoeuvre* (9 June–14 July 1986), a combined Soviet/DRA offensive to clear supply routes to Faizabad in north-eastern Afghanistan, a company from the 783rd Separate Reconnaissance Battalion was to be landed close to the main highway to encircle rebel positions, in a location that had just been cleared by Su-25 strikes. However, a mistaken map reading led to their formation of Mi-8 helicopters heading for a location anything from 8–17km (accounts vary) away from their intended landing zone – and right in the middle of rebel positions. One Mi-8 was shot down with all hands, another was destroyed when lifting out. Fewer than 50 Soviet soldiers found themselves surrounded and came under mortar fire, but attempts to relieve them proved futile until the next day, when Su-25 attack aircraft and Mi-24 gunships were able to be diverted to provide fire support, and the survivors of the 783rd could be lifted out. Twenty-one of the scouts were killed, and none of the rest escaped wounds.

dispensers. Then, on 18 August, a three-day bombing campaign saw the Kokari-Sharshari base hammered by both Su-25s and Su-17s as well as heavy artillery. Meanwhile, helicopters landed the Soviet 201st Motor Rifle Division's 149th Guards Motor Rifle Regiment and detachments from the 345th Airborne Regiment to seize commanding heights along the Harirud Valley, to prevent any reinforcement by rebels based in Iranian territory.

A mix of Soviet and Afghan troops and DRA security forces surrounded the 'green zone' closest to Herat, sealed off the city and began rolling outwards to try to dislodge and eliminate rebel groups and secure key roads. Again, this was done in close integration with the air forces: Mi-24s often led the way, identifying and suppressing rebel ambush sites and concentrations, fixing them for the approaching ground troops. A major of the 5th Motor Rifle Division, who was involved in this stage of the operation, hailed it as 'the best air-land coordination I had yet seen, a battle when things really did work as they should'.

Meanwhile, the assault on Kokari-Sharshari was underway, with 80 per cent of the attacking force having been brought in by helicopter in light of both the desire to strike fast and the extreme difficulty of the terrain. Although there was constant air support for the attack, this was made difficult by both the relief and the location close to the Iranian border. Soviet aircraft operated under very tight controls to ensure they did not accidentally cross into Tehran's airspace, while MiG-23s from the 190th IBAP were on constant patrol, just in case Iranian aircraft sought to intrude, armed with air-to-air loadouts of short-range R-60 and medium-range R-30 missiles.

Helicopters were used constantly for medevac and resupply, although often the geography made this impossible. On the third day, for example, water supplies for some of the assault troops ran out, but attempts to drop rubber drums of drinking water proved impossible – the helicopters were forced to drop them from heights which meant they burst on the ground or ripped on rocks. Eventually, supplies had to be brought in on soldiers' backs. Meanwhile, Su-25 and Su-17 strikes continued day and night, coordinated by an Il-22 aerial command post. Soviet pilots faced carefully planned and interlocking air defences involving HMGs, ZU-23-2 23mm guns, and Blowpipe and Strela-2 MANPADS. One of the former even hit and downed an Su-25 from the 378th OShAP. All the same, the defenders ultimately were not able to prevent the Soviet/DRA force from taking and destroying the base after seven days' hard fighting.

Air power even played a role in the final, urban pacification stage of the operation. Fully 14 battalions were deployed, nine of them Afghan army and security troops, first to seal the neighbourhoods from each other and then to comb them for guerrillas. Sometimes, this led to bitter and destructive firefights, and in several cases Su-25s were called in to launch precision

The impact of the Stinger may have been exaggerated and mythologized, but it did force the Soviets to respond in ways that often hampered their aerial operations. It also created a whole new genre of 'mujahideen with missile' photography, such as this image of a rebel aiming a Stinger at a Soviet aircraft near a rebel base in the Safed Koh Mountains on 10 February 1988. (Robert Nickelsberg/Liaison)

strikes on particular streets and buildings. The Il-22 which had helped manage the air attacks on Kokari-Sharshari was then redirected to help do the same over Herat.

## 4. The 'bleeding wound', 1986–88

General Valentin Varennikov, at the time the Defence Ministry representative in Kabul, described Operation *Trap* as one of the most memorable and successful operations he had witnessed in Afghanistan, but its real significance was back in Moscow. The operation had been as tactically successful as Lieutenant General Dubynin could have hoped – yet the strategic situation was unchanged. This was exactly the kind of lesson Gorbachev wanted in order to bring home to the remaining hardliners quite how futile it was to continue to pour money, men and political capital into Afghanistan.

Just as Western aid to the rebels was reaching its peak – especially with the arrival of the Stingers – Moscow was now eager to scale back its war. Despite the dramatic claims made of the effect of the missiles, what really determined the change in Soviet air tactics was less fear of the new rebel anti-air capability and more a new concern on the part of the Kremlin to minimise costs and casualties at home and prepare the ground for withdrawal. However, this also meant striking a careful balance, keeping the pressure on the various, often bitterly opposed rebel groups to try and give them a reason to reach political deals with the Kabul regime.

## The Stinger

The arrival on the battlefield of the US-made Stinger was as much a political as a military development. It certainly created a new jeopardy for Soviet and DRA pilots, especially at lower altitudes, but it also hammered home Washington's determination to make Moscow

## 'Bring me proof'

At first, there was some suspicion about claims that Washington would provide the *mujahideen* with Stingers, not least because this would inevitably give the Soviets the chance to examine them. On 29 November 1986, in the second known use of the missiles, five were launched against a mixed group of helicopters some 15km north of Jalalabad. An Mi-24 and an Mi-8T were brought down, although one was able to make an emergency landing so the crew could bail out of the burning craft. However, the commander in Jalalabad flatly refused to believe the airmen's account and instead claimed that the two helicopters must have collided, and the pilots were simply covering for each other. He demanded proof of these mystery missiles. Nonetheless, he was prevailed on to allow a mission to look for evidence, and the 2nd battalion of the 66th Motor Rifle Brigade and the 1st company of the 154th OSN quartered the area of the crash. Finding nothing that proved anything in the burnt-out ruins of the two helicopters, they then went and explored the probable launch sites. There, they found the discarded launch tubes of five Stinger missiles, providing the first clear evidence of this escalation – and exonerating the flight crews. The company commander who found them ended up being awarded the Order of the Red Banner.

suffer so long as it prosecuted the war. Ironically, in that respect it was helping to make Gorbachev's point for him. In the immediate moment, though, it was a technical and tactical challenge which the 40th Army needed to address – at least once it believed that Stingers had actually been deployed (see box).

The first and most straightforward move was to order aircraft not to launch strikes from below 4,500m, a floor which was eventually raised to 7,500m. As Daoud Rams, a defector from the DRA Air Force who had flown MiG-21s, said: 'Before Stinger, we were free to do almost anything we wanted. After Stinger was introduced, we changed all our tactics, altitudes and speed – everything. We did not like to fly down low, and when we had to, we flew very fast, and even at high altitudes, we flew as fast as we could… We were no longer able to operate at will whenever and wherever we wanted to.' This somewhat over-stated the impact, although arguably the DRA adopted an even more cautious approach than the Soviets, but it certainly speaks to the psychological impact of this new weapon. Of course, flying higher reduced the accuracy of attacks, so in practice more aircraft had to launch more sorties and drop more ordnance to have the same operational impact. This was not practical for helicopters, although sometimes they would adopt ground-hugging approaches, compared with the previous 'high-and-dive' tactics, which would have left them dangerously exposed to MANPADS lock-on. Thus, there was a rapid programme to fit them with new countermeasures designed to spoof, decoy and blind a Stinger's IR seeker warhead. Ever since 1983, they had already had baffles on their engine nozzles to reduce the signature, and more were fitted with ASO-2V flare dispensers (that could also scatter clouds of radar-jamming chaff) and SOEP-V1A Lipa active jammers.

Not content with relying purely on such passive measures, the 40th Army also stepped up its use of *Spetsnaz* long-range raids and ambushes to intercept caravans believed to be bringing Stingers to the rebels. This was, after all, simply an extension of existing efforts. Just in 1987, for example, 332 arms caravans were reported as having been intercepted, leading to the destruction or capture of more than 290 various heavy weapons, from mortars to HMGs, 80 MANPADS (mainly Hunyin-5), more than 15,000 mines and about 8 million rounds of small arms ammunition. The aim of the 'Stinger hunts' was not to prevent any missiles from making it in – that would have been an impossible task – but to slow their spread and give the technicians back home more time to devise countermeasures.

The first to be seized were two found when the reconnaissance company of the 66th Separate Motor Rifle Brigade under Senior Lieutenant Igor Ryumtsev took a rebel arms dump outside Jalalabad on 26 December 1986. At first, they didn't even know what the two tubes they had found were, but soon the hunt for Stingers became more deliberate, aided by the rumour that whoever first captured one would be made a Hero of the Soviet Union. On

As the threat of rebel MANPADS became a greater concern, sights like this became more common, of Mi-24s firing flares to distract their heat-seeking heads. (Maxim Guchek/BELTA/AFP via Getty Images)

5 January 1987, Senior Lieutenant Vladimir Kovtun's *Spetsnaz* team from the 186th Special Designation Detachment (OSN: *Otryad Spetsialnovo Naznacheniya*) were on a helicopter patrol when they noted some rebels fleeing on motorcycles. They engaged and the rebels fired two Stingers, which missed because they had not waited to ensure a lock-on. They didn't have the chance to launch any more, as the commandos engaged them from the ground and another pair of Mi-24 gunships attacked from the air. When Kovtun investigated, as well as the two launchers, he found another missile, and – a particularly useful prize – a briefcase containing the technical manuals. In the next few months, five more missiles would be seized which did indeed give the Soviets the opportunity to take them apart and study them in detail.

Kovtun never did become a Hero of the Soviet Union. In 2012, Yevgeny Sergeyev, who at the time had been commander of the 186th OSN, was made a Hero of Russia, but even that was four years after his death.

## Operation *Highway*, 1987–88

To maintain the balance between wasting resources on the war and losing it, the 40th Army realised it needed to maintain the DRA's credibility with its core constituency, the urban population. No cities could be allowed to fall. In summer 1987, though, rebels had begun to block the main road from Gardez to Khost, the largest city in the south-east of the country. The 40,000-strong population and DRA garrison of 8,000 was virtually cut off by a force of more than 10,000 *mujahideen*, and morale was understandably plummeting. Although there was consideration of an airlift, this was discounted as no more than an expensive palliative. Instead, the decision was made to mount a major ground offensive to reopen the road to Khost, an operation that was imaginatively named *Magistral*, or *Highway*.

The operation involved a joint Soviet/DRA force spearheaded by the 108th Motor Rifle Division but was also marked by the increasingly confident use of coordinated air and ground

operations and air assaults. The attack had to pass through the heavily defended Satukandav Pass, for example, and in order to force the *mujahideen* to show their hand, then Lieutenant General Boris Gromov, the operational commander, ordered dummy paratroopers, just sandbags wrapped in parachute harnesses, dropped at the mouth of the pass. Believing this to be an attack, the rebels opened up with everything they had – all of which was carefully tracked by reconnaissance aircraft, likely a pair of Yak-28Rs. This allowed the Soviets to then respond with a strike by Su-25 aircraft using rockets, bombs and, for a change, laser-guided

Soviet *razvedchiki*, reconnaissance troops, in KLMK camouflage overalls, preparing for a mission after being landed by helicopter. (ZUMA Press, Inc./Alamy)

Lieutenant General Boris Gromov was one of the stars of the war, especially once the Soviet propaganda machine had pivoted from trying to pretend it wasn't happening to making what gains it could from it. Photographed at a press conference in Kabul the day before the final Soviet withdrawal, he wears under his jacket the *telnyashka*, the striped blue-and-white vest of the airborne forces. (Robert Nickelsberg/Getty Images)

**OPPOSITE** MULTI-LEVEL BOMBING OPERATION

Kh-25ML (NATO: AS-10) missiles, taking advantage of the unusually fresh targeting data. This was followed up by a lengthy artillery barrage.

Nonetheless, the advance was difficult as the rebels were well entrenched and numerous. Again, though, air power proved crucial, allowing Gromov to send both Soviet paratroopers and Afghan commandos onto commanding heights along the way and force the *mujahideen* to retreat or face encirclement. Three times this approach was used, with the helicopters virtually acting, as Gromov put it, as '*marshrutkas* on circuit', comparing them with the shared minibus taxis that followed regular routes in Soviet cities.

On 30 December, the route to Khost was opened, and although supply convoys on the road would still come under regular attack, a combination of temporary outposts along its length and regular helicopter patrols essentially managed to keep it open. Khost was secure, at least for a while – and the risk of the rebels not only managing for the first time to take a city, but also establishing an urban base close to the border with Pakistan, had been averted.

## 5. Withdrawal, 1988–89

Once the withdrawal from Afghanistan had started, the 40th Army command under General Gromov had to juggle three sometimes contradictory priorities. The withdrawal had to be orderly, and on the agreed schedule, which required a relatively early retreat from the south of the country, including Kandahar, as well as a substantial tranche of

## Rutskoi's war

Alexander Rutskoi, with Boris Gromov, became one of the most widely recognized heroes of the Soviet war. He likewise became a political figure afterwards, both because of his own ambitions and because others wanted to harness an Afghan war hero to their cause. A fighter-bomber pilot, he transferred to the Su-25, and having risen to the rank of lieutenant colonel, he was commanding the 378th OShAP on 6 April 1986 when, on his 360th combat mission, he was leading a four-plane attack on the heavily defended rebel base at Zhawar. He was hit on his second pass (he was flying a camera-equipped plane for battle damage assessment) by a FIM-43 Redeye. He ended up ejecting at dangerously low altitude and thus suffered a serious spinal compression fracture on hitting the ground. A DRA APC managed to evacuate him, but only after a firefight which left him with two more wounds, in the leg and back. He was medevaced by Soviet helicopter to Kabul where doctors warned him that his flying days were over and he was likely to spend the rest of his life in a wheelchair. Nonetheless, Rutskoi was nothing if not determined, and within two months was walking on crutches. Although he was assigned a non-combat position, he was determined to get back to *Afgan*, and in April 1988 he returned, a full colonel and deputy commander of the 40th Army's aviation. Nonetheless, he continued to fly combat missions, and reportedly was even more daring and aggressive than before.

In April–August 1988, he flew 97 sorties, 48 of them at night, but his luck ran out on 4 August when he was leading a night-time attack on a rebel ammunition depot that Moscow claims was near the village of Shaboheil, just south of Khost. This was less than 7km from the Pakistani border, and to avoid the risk of confliction, Soviet aircraft were banned from flying within 5km of the frontier. On the other hand, Pakistan claims the sortie was against a facility at Miran Shah, inside its territory. Either way, Rutskoi's Su-25 was engaged and shot down by a Pakistani F-16A with an AIM-9L Sidewinder missile and he parachuted onto Pakistani territory.

He managed to evade capture for five days but was eventually taken prisoner of war. He was released two weeks later in a prisoner exchange after intense diplomatic pressure as well as the direct intervention of KGB foreign intelligence chief Viktor Kryuchkov. That was the end of his combat flying, but he was made a Hero of the Soviet Union and later would be elected to the Congress of People's Deputies and stood as vice president on Boris Yeltsin's ticket. Yeltsin essentially wanted him just for the lustre of his hero's star, though, and the two men soon fell out. In 1993, Rutskoi was a key figure opposing Yeltsin in a constitutional crisis between parliament and president that turned into an armed clash and led to parliament being shelled into submission. Rutskoi was sacked, but would later be elected governor of the Kursk region 1996–2000.

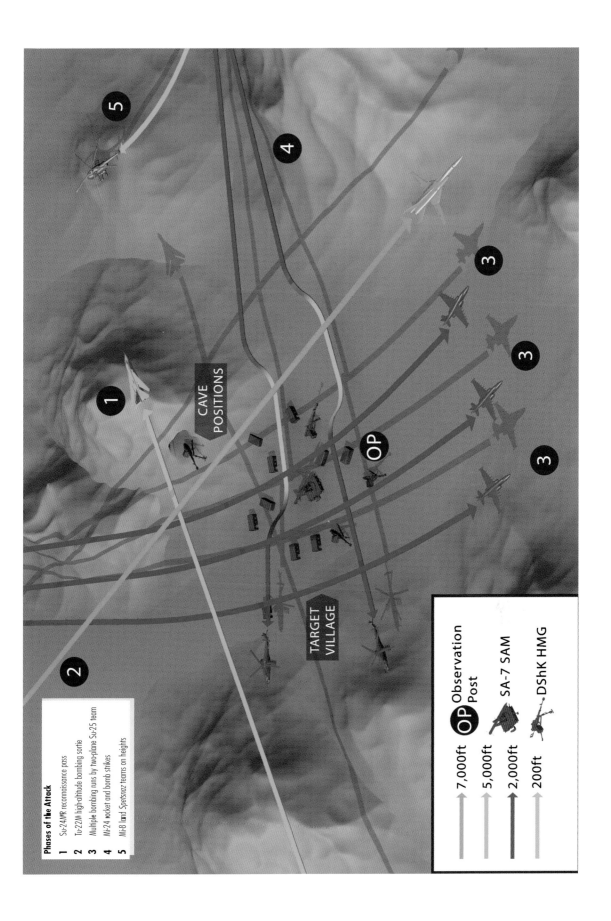

**Phases of the Attack**

1  Su-24MR reconnaissance pass
2  Tu-22M high-altitude bombing sortie
3  Multiple bombing runs by two-plane Su-25 team
4  Mi-24 rocket and bomb strikes
5  Mi-8 land *Spetsnaz* teams on heights

CAVE POSITIONS

TARGET VILLAGE

OP

**Observation Post**

SA-7 SAM

DShK HMG

7,000ft

5,000ft

2,000ft

200ft

Lionized during the war and then courted after it, Alexander Rutskoi then became a leader of the anti-Yeltsin forces during the 1993 Russian constitutional crisis. (Chuck Nacke/Alamy)

A suitably staged photo of an Afghan pilot shaking hands with a Soviet soldier as they say goodbye on 13 February 1989 at Kabul airport. In fact, many of the DRA's soldiers felt betrayed by the withdrawal. (Reuters/Richard Ellis)

forces, including air units. It also had to be as free of casualties as possible and not to convey panic. The Politburo, after all, was desperate to avoid the kind of optics that had accompanied the US retreat from Vietnam, with helicopters frantically evacuating from the embassy roof, and excess aircraft being tipped from the deck of an aircraft carrier. Finally,

# Bad blood

Relations between the Soviet and Afghan forces had always been complex. There were many cases of good cooperation and strong, friendly relations, especially given how many DRA officers had studied in the USSR. There was, however, often also a strong undercurrent of casual racism on the Soviets' part, and resentment by the Afghans that they did not receive the same kit or support. This was especially true between the air forces, not just because the disparity in equipment was most striking, but also because the Soviets were frequently infuriated by what they saw as their counterparts' indolence and refusal to put themselves at risk. DRA pilots for much of the war might only fly a few sorties a week, while Soviets routinely flew several every day, for example. Whatever the rights and wrongs, this created fertile grounds for tensions once it became clear that the 40th Army was leaving. Afghan airmen began refusing to fly in support of Soviet troops or calling their counterparts 'traitors' or 'cowards'. Defections became more common: in 1988–89, nine DRA aircraft ended up in Pakistan, claiming asylum. So too did sabotage directed against the Soviets, such as leaving debris on taxiways or even slashing hydraulic lines. Increasingly, the security troops of the Separate Guard Battalions took to further limiting Afghans' access to Soviet parts of airbases, further exacerbating tensions in a vicious circle of mistrust.

adequate support had to be given the DRA to ensure it did not collapse when or right after the Soviets left. The problem was that supporting the DRA and deterring attacks on the withdrawing forces meant active combat operations, especially by the air forces – and that risked casualties.

Although the phased rotation out of certain units deemed redundant, including the last anti-aircraft missile regiments and tank regiments, had been completed in 1986, the General Staff's Main Planning Directorate was only formally instructed to draw up a comprehensive plan for the withdrawal of the OKSVA in early 1988. Nonetheless, preliminary work had been underway for some time, so they were quickly ready. The overall plan was formally agreed by Defence Minister Dmitry Yazov on 7 April and entrusted to an Operations Group set up within the General Staff under Lieutenant General Alfred Gaponenko. It was tasked with managing the withdrawal in conjunction with the 40th Army command staff. Gaponenko had been the head of the Soviet advisers mission in Laos during the Vietnam war, and was especially aware of the risks if the morale of the DRA's forces began to collapse.

The operation would thus be staged. About half the 110,000-strong OKSVA would leave between 15 May and 15 August 1988 as well as the lion's share of the 120,000 other Soviets in-country at the time, who ranged from Motor-Manoeuvre Groups from the KGB Border Troops and elements of the Ministry of Internal Affairs Interior Troops, through intelligence specialists and technicians attached to combat repair units, to all kinds of civilians, including teachers, engineers, administrators and families. The second stage between 1 September 1988 and 15 February 1989 would be trickier, as it entailed the staged withdrawal of the last units without screening forces – except those of the DRA, on whom no one truly wanted to rely – and that through the harsh Afghan winter. This would depend all the more heavily on air power, increasingly projected from Soviet airbases, to provide intelligence on rebel advances, deterrent against potential attacks, and a devastating and rapid response when that failed.

## Punching the MiG-27's card

However, even while plans were being made for withdrawal, there were those desperate to get to *Afgan*. If for most conscripts, being sent to Afghanistan was a terror (and hence many would gladly pay bribes to avoid it), the career soldiers would often actively seek to serve a tour there. 'Punching your card' with genuine combat service – and quite possibly getting some kind of medal – was an invaluable boost to your chances of promotion, and the markets and *voyentorg* PX stores in Afghanistan held goods that were near-impossible to find in a

The distinctive chisel nose of the MiG-27 set this ground-attack aircraft apart from the MiG-23 fighter from which it was derived. (Peter Lane/ Alamy)

bankrupt USSR. The final year of the war thus saw many officers jostle for the final chances to see action. This also applied to airframes.

The MiG-27 fighter-bomber was amongst the largest and most capable aircraft in the Soviet air fleet, yet had not seen combat duty in its first decade and a half in service. For years, whenever it had been mooted that it could be deployed in Afghanistan, the decision always went against. The Su-17, nicknamed *strizh*, or 'swift', had, after all, proven a reliable workhorse, and sticking to the same aircraft year after year, even if supplemented with new variants, dramatically simplified the maintenance, supply and planning of fighter-bomber operations.

In autumn 1988, as it was time for another rotation of airframes (given the wear and tear from active service), and once again the question of deploying the MiG-27 arose. After all, there were more than two dozen regiments of them in use, and with withdrawal on the way, why waste one last opportunity to give them a proper work-out in genuine combat conditions? The idea was taken up enthusiastically by the pilots and officers from MiG-27 regiments, who had long envied the opportunities enjoyed by their counterparts flying 'swifts'. They found a sympathetic ear in Major General Dmitry Romanyuk, head of the 40th Army's air forces since 1986 – and the former commander of a MiG-27 squadron in the Transbaikal Military District.

The early withdrawal of Soviet forces from Kandahar on 15 August had taken a bite out of the 40th Army's air wing, and while some craft were moved to Shindand, the fighter-bomber fleet was overburdened. This gave Romanyuk, and the MiG-27 lobby in the neighbouring Central Asian Military District, the opportunity to present the move as a necessary qualitative upgrade.

The 134th IBAP was chosen to be deployed, although, as it would leave behind its newest and least experienced pilots, it was supplemented by a squadron transferred from the 129th IBAP. The advanced MiG-27K with a high-specification electro-optic sensor suite was most highly regarded by its pilots, but there was a sense that its systems would be of little value in the difficult terrain where it would be used, especially at the elevated altitudes the presence of Stingers forced on the fighter-bombers. Thus, they were equipped with MiG-27D and MiG-27M aircraft, which had gone through the usual modifications

to cope with the Afghan combat environment, with flare dispensers and tweaks to the engine management system to handle the hot and rarefied mountain air.

After mountain orientation training at Kyzyl-Agash in Kazakhstan and the issue of camouflage coveralls and self-defence weapons, the regiment deployed to Shindand, an airbase that by this time had expanded to a total strength of almost 9,000 personnel – while the local settlement just held something like 5,000 Afghans. From there, the 134th IBAP conducted operations across the country, including in the Herat and Farah regions, but primarily around Kandahar in support of the beleaguered remaining forces there.

Typically, 16 MiG-27s would be deployed per shift, flying three or four sorties each, equipped with a mix of bombs including ZAB-100-175 and ZAB-250-200 incendiaries, and even the ODAB-500 and ODAB-500P thermobarics, although the latter were considered deadly but temperamental. They generally did not carry the rocket pods or missiles with which they could be fitted, because by this point the High Command regarded avoiding losses to be a priority, and to use them properly, the aircraft would have to descend to ranges at which they would be vulnerable to AA fire or missiles. As a result, the levels of accuracy were never going to be especially impressive, considering the munitions were all 'dumb' bombs, and the pilots had largely trained for different kinds of operations.

Nonetheless, as *Spetsnaz* patrols were withdrawn and helicopter operations concentrated on protecting withdrawing forces, the MiG-27s were able to play a significant role in day and night missions to interdict rebel supply caravans. Although most fighter-bombers were due to leave Shindand on 27 January, handing over remaining duties to squadrons flying out of airbases on the Soviet side of the border, the 134th IBAP stayed until the end of the month to fly a final range of missions against rebel supply lines. They then relocated to the Kalai-Mor airbase in Turkmenistan, in case there was a need for an eleventh-hour relief of Kabul, before returning to their home base in March.

The pilots of the 134th IBAP certainly got their chance of combat experience. In their 95 days of deployment, each logged, on average, 70–80 sorties and 60–70 hours' flight time. The logbook of Captain Vladimir Pravdivets, for example, shows him as having dropped 36,250kg of bombs. Likewise, the MiG-27 got its combat test, proving to be a reliable

Soviet MiG-27 pilots after a mission in 1980. (Universal History Archive/ Universal Images Group via Getty Images)

aircraft and effective, considering the mismatch between this conflict and the type of war it was designed to fight, even if it was thirsty and demanded longer runways than some of its simpler counterparts.

## Operation *Air-Bridge*, January–February 1989

A sign of the kind of challenges the withdrawal would bring was the siege of Kandahar after the Soviets had handed its security to the DRA forces as part of a wide draw-down in the southern Helmand and Kandahar provinces in August 1988. Emboldened, the rebels quickly took control of most of the territory, but the city of Kandahar, the second largest in the country, remained in government hands. To keep it supplied and thus standing, the Soviets mounted their last major operation in the south, codenamed rather uncryptically *Vozdushny Most*, or *Air-Bridge*.

The Soviets had maintained a cantonment in Kandahar that included government buildings, the airport, warehouses and the barracks of the 70th Separate Motor Rifle Brigade. These, along with large stocks of ammunition, were transferred to the DRA's 2nd Corps, under Lieutenant General Nur-ul-Haq Ulumi. For all its impressive title, though, his 'army corps' really only comprised some 1,500 soldiers, although it was reinforced by a tank battalion from the 7th Armoured Brigade as well as elements from the KhAD and the Interior Ministry's Sarandoy security troops.

This was still a reasonably effective fighting force, but the *mujahideen* plan was to starve them out. They swept away the remaining small outposts outside the city limits, then closed first the road leading to Kabul and then the one connecting Kandahar to the Soviet border and the city of Kushka, which had been a key source of supplies. The DRA government urgently petitioned Moscow for help, and given that the Politburo's goal was to try and ensure the regime survived at least long enough to avoid embarrassment, the Soviets agreed.

Initially, the plan was to drive a supply convoy overland from Kushka, via Herat, to Kandahar, spearheaded by either the 15th *Spetsnaz* Brigade or the 56th Separate Guards Air Assault Brigade. However, in October, the Soviets had launched Operation *Dam*, a similar mission to push a 2,000-vehicle convoy to another besieged DRA garrison at the town of Kajaki, who were guarding a hydroelectric power station on the Helmand River. It took the

After the Soviet withdrawal, military and food aid continued to flow from the USSR. Here, an Afghan worker unloads food supplies from a Soviet transport at Kabul airport, in March 1989. (Derrick Ceyrac/ AFP via Getty Images)

5th Guards Motor Rifle Division two full weeks of hard fighting to battle their way to Kajaki, with the loss of many of the supply trucks on the way, and eventually it was decided that it made more sense simply to withdraw the government troops.

No one at the 40th Army headquarters had the stomach to try to repeat Operation *Dam*, especially as it was estimated that between Gulbuddin Hekmatyar's Islamic Party of Afghanistan and other, smaller local rebel forces, there were some 10,000 guerrillas in and across the region, and they had already mined the main roads

Although the Mi-24D was the main version of this gunship deployed in Afghanistan, some use was made of the later Mi-24P, which mounts a side-mounted 30mm GSh-30-2K twin-barrel autocannon. (Eric Bouvet/Gamma-Rapho via Getty Images)

extensively. Instead, the decision was made to launch a massive aerial resupply operation, under the direct command of Major General Nikolai Pishchev, the 40th Army's First Deputy Commander.

Kandahar's Ariana airport was, nonetheless, deemed both insecure and lacking proper air traffic control. As a result, the first Soviet An-12 flights on the morning of 20 January 1989 brought not only a company of scouts from the 5th Guards Motor Rifle Division's 650th Battalion, but also an R-440 satellite communication system that was quickly set up to allow the arrival of the next wave of transports. Despite rebel shelling and even attempts to breach the defensive perimeter, on the first day alone, 28 sorties were flown from the Mary airfield in Soviet Turkmenistan and four flights from Shindand, together delivering 326 tonnes of cargo, of which 240 were artillery ammunition. In addition, the airport protection detail was reinforced with another platoon from the 650th Battalion and six BTR-60PB APCs, with the thought that in a worst-case scenario, at the end of the operation the remaining troops on the ground could use them to break through the enemy lines and drive to Shindand, even though in practice this would have been a near-suicidal run.

As the supply flights continued, the rebels stepped up mortar and rocket attacks in an attempt to close the runway. On 23 January, an An-12 was hit as it was landing and seriously damaged, with a total of 31 rockets hitting the airfield that day. That evening, rebels even tried to infiltrate the airfield, although they were driven off by ground troops. Nonetheless, the flow of cargo was partially interrupted: whereas 212 tonnes of supplies were brought in by 37 flights the day before, this fell to 173 tonnes in 17 sorties on the 23rd.

# High-altitude bombing, 1982

The Tu-22M bomber provided a powerful asset to the Soviets, able to hit anywhere in the country from bases in the Soviet Union, and stay high enough to be immune from any rebel AA. Here, two Tu-22M bombers from the 185th Guards Heavy Bomber Aviation Regiment are flying an early morning bombing sortie over the Panjshir Valley. It is 16 May 1982, the start of the large-scale Operation Panjshir V, and they are unloading full loads of FAB-500 M-54 bombs before returning to base. The bomber in the background is clearly in a hurry to get back to the comforts of base, and has begun to bank even as its last bombs leave its internal bomb bay. Especially in the early years, pilots too often seemed less interested in accurate bombing runs than in completing their missions as quickly as possible. Nonetheless, considering they flew at altitudes typically of 10,000m or more and relied on often out-of-date or inaccurate targeting data, whether this had much of an impact in practice is open to question.

The MiG-29 fighter was one of the most advanced aircraft in the Soviet arsenal, and was only deployed as an occasional escort to long-range bomber sorties at the end of the war, primarily in case they were intercepted by the Pakistani Air Force. (USAF)

Next, the *mujahideen* attacked not the airport but the warehouses holding the supplies, and managed to destroy one holding 300 tonnes of ammunition, in effect negating a day and a half of dangerous supply flights. In some ways though, this was a pyrrhic victory as it pushed the Soviets into launching a series of air strikes to punish the rebels and degrade their capabilities of attacking Kandahar. Su-25s from the 378th OShAP, Su-17s from the 274th IBAP and MiG-27s from the 134th IBAP were all deployed, with support from MiG-23MLDs from the 120th IAP. While the Su-25s flew low attacks – one pilot involved admitted that they often ignored the official minimum altitudes imposed because of the presence of Stingers, in order to allow them to strike rocket and mortar positions with accuracy – the other aircraft maintained a steady tempo of suppression operations for several days. Furthermore, Tu-22M3s of the 185th TBAP under Colonel Dzhokar Dudayev (see box) flew a single sortie to hit the rebel command post in the village of Daman, 10km north of the airport, with 3-tonne FAB-3000 demolition bombs.

The effect was to reduce the density of incoming artillery fire onto the airport and deter any ground attacks, and by 1 February some 2,600 tonnes of supplies had been delivered to the embattled Kandahar garrison. However, serious dust storms then forced the Soviets to stop the relief flights until 3 February. In that period, the 40th Army command decided that honour had been satisfied, and on the evening of the 3rd ordered the immediate withdrawal of the Soviets in Kandahar. Even though the dust storms were still blowing, that night six An-12s evacuated all 170 Soviet soldiers and technicians at Ariana, under heavy enemy fire. The 650th Battalion's heavy weapons and vehicles were left with the DRA garrison

## Dudayev's war

Another of the participants of the Afghan War who would end up playing a disproportionate – and disruptive – role in Russian politics was Colonel Dzhokar Dudayev. He was an ethnic Chechen born in 1944, in the immediate aftermath of Stalin's brutal deportation of his whole people to Siberia and Central Asia. Nonetheless, like so many Chechens, out of both economic necessity and a warrior culture, he joined the Soviet military. Finding himself in the DA, he rose as a bomber commander, with a reputation for being prickly and quick-tempered, yet also painfully honest. By 1989, he was commanding the 326th Tarnopol Heavy Bomber Division of the 46th Strategic Air Army in Estonia, and when a squadron of Tu-22M3s of the 185th TBAP was temporarily deployed to Mary airbase for operations in Afghanistan, he led the deployment. Although his critics later claimed he was guilty of 'carpet bombing', in fact his squadron was involved in more selective and targeted strikes. This did his career no harm at all, netting him the Order of the Red Banner and promotion to the rank of major general. Soon after, he became involved in Chechen politics, though, and he would later become president of the self-declared independent Chechen Republic in the Russian North Caucasus. In a poignant irony, he died in 1996 during the First Chechen War as a result of a Russian airstrike.

which, suitably resupplied, would now hold out until the eventual fall of Najibullah's regime. The Soviets lost one An-12BP transport from the 930th VTAP and an An-26M *Spasitel* ambulance aircraft from the 50th OSAP, but suffered no fatalities throughout the entire operation, despite a rain of some 700 rockets and shells and an unknown number of mortar bombs. More to the point, thanks to this resupply – and the reminder of the Soviet will to support DRA forces *in extremis* – Lieutenant General Ulumi was able to hold Kandahar, not least by making pragmatic alliances with local rebel groups. Once again, Soviet air power proved crucial in shaping the facts on the ground, and thus the political calculations they drove.

## 'Rolling down the stocking'

The war that had once been taboo in the Soviet media had become a spectacle, and with a metaphor a number of commanders would later also use, the Soviet TV commentator Mikhail Leshinsky described the second stage of the withdrawal, which began on 15 August, as 'rolling down the Soviet forces along the route (of disengagement) like a stocking'. This was a dangerous phase. Some rebel commanders were willing to save their ammunition for later, willing to let the operation go essentially unhindered. Others were looking for one last chance to punish the *Shuravi* or wanted to move quickly to fill the vacuum they would leave. With radicals like Gulbuddin Hekmatyar manoeuvring to steal a march on their rivals, even more pragmatic figures such as Ahmad Shah Massoud felt under pressure to act, lest they give their rivals an open path to Kabul and power.

In this explosive political and military environment, the Soviets turned to liberal use of air power to clear their withdrawal routes and hammer any rebel forces which looked likely to try and make a hostile move. Even Massoud's Panjshir, with which the 40th Army had been able to reach an understanding of sorts (much to Najibullah's disgust), got a precautionary battering in the controversial Operation *Typhoon*, a major air and artillery assault that was

A Tupolev Tu-16 bomber was an ageing but still effective design, used repeatedly over Afghanistan. Here, one on a maritime recon-strike mission is escorted by US Navy fighters over the North Pacific Ocean in January 1963. (© Museum of Flight/CORBIS/Corbis via Getty Images)

purely punitive and disruptive in its intent. Another of the high-profile *Afgantsy*, paratrooper Colonel Valery Vostrotin, who had been made a Hero of the Soviet Union for his exploits in the war, was especially bitter at this betrayal of the deal, calling it 'dishonourable… We just despicably destroyed them.'

Nonetheless, the air attacks continued. The aim was as much as anything else disruption, to prevent the rebels from concentrating and to obstruct supply caravans. To this end, Su-17s from the 274th IBAP began flying night sorties not just in pairs and links but in groups as large as 16 or even 24 aircraft. Su-24s were also deployed in growing numbers, and were even better suited to night operations. These raids were supplemented by increased use of heavy bombers. In autumn 1988, a special DA task force was established specifically to cover the retreat, including Tu-16s of the 251st Guards TBAP from Bila Tserkva and two squadrons of Tu-22M3s from the 185th Guards TBAP from Poltava. They were used to bomb sites around Kabul from which the rebels were launching nightly rocket attacks on the capital, although the rebels soon took to mounting their improvised launch rails on pickup trucks and quickly switching locations to avoid reprisal counter-battery fire from the Kabul garrison and airstrikes. However, their main targets were around Kandahar and Jalalabad, which the Soviets had already abandoned. There they could often operate with less constraint, and Tu-16s began to use massive FAB-9000 M-54 bombs, which required the installation of special holding braces in their bomb bays. In just three months, the Tu-16s dropped 289 of these 9-tonne, 5m-long brutes, which one flight crewman described as a 'barrel full of hell'. While in some ways ill-suited to these operations, because they were really designed to level large urban structures and were thus wasted erasing Afghan villages, the very scale of their blast was powerful as a psychological weapon as much as anything else. Furthermore, the crews came to realize they were especially effective when dropped in gorges, where the valley sides reflected the blast.

Unlike most Soviet aircraft, the Tu-16s were generally sent out in threes, accompanied by MiG-29 or occasionally MiG-23 or Su-17 escorts. The Tu-22M3s tended to fly in pairs, but larger raids might be accompanied by a Tu-22PD electronic warfare version, as there was a serious concern, albeit one which never materialized, that Pakistan might step up its aerial operations over the border. The bombers flew virtually to the very last minute of the occupation, and although Najibullah requested a continued campaign after the withdrawal, the Politburo refused. Nonetheless, the bombers stayed at Mary for another three weeks in case of any catastrophic setback in Afghanistan, before finally heading home.

A Pakistani F-16BM in flight. The arrival of F-16s, which dramatically improved the Pakistani Air Force's interceptor capabilities, led to a newly assertive approach towards Soviet operations near or over its borders. (Asuspine)

# AFTERMATH AND ANALYSIS

This was not a war which could have been won by Soviet air power – but it could well have been lost without it. It proved to be a vital force multiplier for the relatively limited forces the Politburo was willing to deploy. After all, at peak, in 1986, the OKSVA only reached 109,000 personnel, fewer than 0.7 per square kilometre of the country, compared with the peak US deployment to Vietnam in 1969, when there were more than 1.6 per square kilometre. This was, from the first, a war fought on the cheap, in which the Soviet leadership, except for a brief time under Chernenko, was more interested in minimizing costs than winning a military victory.

In that context, air power was often deployed in ways that frustrated the airmen themselves. The hot-headed Alexander Rutskoi rhetorically asked: 'Why fly, burn kerosene, and drop hundreds of tonnes of expensive ammunition per day, if the effectiveness of the strikes is going to be zero?' This was, though, in many ways to understate the value of the air campaign, which was as much about disrupting rebel attacks and heartening DRA forces as actually winning battles. An army major who served in the 40th Army in 1987–88 was candid about this: 'Whatever they may have done on the battlefield, the greatest value of our aircraft was in reminding everyone, friend and foe, what we *could* do.'

## A balance sheet

The Soviets lost some 333 helicopters and 125 fixed-wing aircraft over Afghanistan, to accident and enemy action. This was, of course, a terrible toll, especially when the pilots and aircrews who also died are considered. By comparison, though, the Vietnam War, while twice as long, took a far larger bite of US air assets: more than 3,700 aircraft and 5,600 helicopters. This is not to draw any direct comparison between the respective militaries – the Americans were fighting not just insurgents but also a determined nation-state enemy with all the air and anti-air capabilities that entails. They were also fighting the war a different way. Rather,

The Il-76 was the mainstay of strategic Soviet troop airlift. This one, photographed bringing soldiers back from Kabul airport, is in the livery of Aeroflot, the Soviet flag airline, but would likely be operating with military aircrew from the VTA. (Patrick Robert/Sygma via Getty Images)

Marshal Sergei Akhromeyev was one of the outstanding officers of his generation, who played a key role in planning the invasion of Afghanistan in 1979 and was Chief of the General Staff for much of the war (1984–88). (Russian MOD)

it is to highlight the relatively limited nature of the conflict, the Soviet commitment and thus their losses.

| Soviet and DRA helicopter losses in Afghanistan (combat and accident) | | | |
|---|---|---|---|
| | Soviet | DRA | Total |
| Mi-6 | 28 | | 28 |
| Mi-8 (all variants) | 174 | 233 | 407 |
| Mi-10 | 1 | | 1 |
| Mi-24 (all variants) | 129 | 72 | 201 |
| N/A | 1 | 33 | 34 |
| Total | 333 | 338 | 671 |

The war was not won, but one can debate whether or not it was truly lost, either. The generals, when asked what force levels they would need to win, suggested half a million troops and four times as many aircraft, something the Politburo would never countenance. The losses were bearable, even in the context of the decaying Soviet economy, and the political fallout likewise. It was air power, though, that made the difference. To quote General Rodionov, the former 40th Army commander who went on briefly to become defence minister: 'Without the "turntables" [helicopters] and "rooks" [Su-25s], we would have needed twice as many men to accomplish half as much.'

| Soviet fixed-wing aircraft losses in Afghanistan (combat and accident) | | | | | | | | | | | | |
|---|---|---|---|---|---|---|---|---|---|---|---|---|
| | 1979 | 1980 | 1981 | 1982 | 1983 | 1984 | 1985 | 1986 | 1987 | 1988 | 1989 | Total |
| An-12 | | | | | 3 | 2 | 1 | 1 | 2 | | 1 | 10 |
| An-26 | | | | | | | 1 | 1 | 2 | 1 | 1 | 6 |
| An-30 | | | | | | 1 | | | | | | 1 |
| Il-76 | 1 | | | | 1 | | | | | | | 2 |
| MiG-21 | | 6 | 1 | 7 | 2 | 5 | | | | | | 21 |
| MiG-23 | | | | | | 5 | | 3 | 2 | 1 | | 11 |
| Su-17 | | 1 | 2 | 1 | 3 | 8 | 3 | 9 | 4 | 3 | | 34 |
| Su-24 | | | | | | | | | 1 | | | 1 |
| Su-25 | | | 1 | | 1 | 4 | 1 | 8 | 8 | 12 | 1 | 36 |
| Yak-28 | | 1 | | | | | | | 1 | | | 2 |
| Total | 1 | 7 | 5 | 8 | 9 | 20 | 12 | 19 | 20 | 19 | 4 | 124 |

# Adaptation

Despite its often hidebound appearance, the Soviet military proved an effective learning organization, even if sometimes in informal ways, at odds with its official practice. For a variety of reasons, the General Staff did not undertake a single, definitive analysis, as it had of past wars. In part, this may have been because, as discussed below, it was regarded as a regrettable one-off, in part because of ideological discomfort about a war in which they were the imperial power, but above all because of the turmoil into which the USSR was descending by the time of the withdrawal. That said, many military educational institutions and research centres did conduct their own studies, from the Voroshilov Military Academy of the General Staff to the 30th Order of the Red Star Central Research Institute, which specialized in aviation matters.

Some of this fed into the technical adaptations made, from improving how helicopter engines could cope with Afghan conditions to developing countermeasures to MANPADS.

An Mi-24 escorts an Il-76 troop transport as it leaves Kabul airport on 6 February 1989, firing flares to distract any rebel SAM attacks. (Eric Bouvet/ Gamma-Rapho via Getty Images)

There were also tactical and organizational responses that originated in such research, such as the practice of using parachute flares at night to blind rebel gunners or the evolving notions of how helicopters could be integrated into the work of the Assault Landing Brigade (DShB).

Arguably, though, many of the most important innovations came from the experiences in-theatre. Like the army, for example, the air forces gained a new appreciation of the importance in inculcating a sense of initiative in its officers, and a willingness to give them a degree of tactical flexibility. They came to realize that a system which for so long had been based on large units operating under a rigid hierarchy doesn't work in counter-insurgency. For example, the concept of the 'free hunt', when a pair or link of aircraft were given an area in which to operate and left largely to their own devices was not wholly new – the original Il-2 *Shturmovik* attack aircraft had practised something similar during World War II – but it was taken to a new level in Afghanistan.

## Protecting the Mi-6

The lumbering Mi-6 was an invaluable heavy-lift helicopter, but also a prize target for rebel MANPADS operators and a vulnerable one at that. Considerable effort was made to protect it from rebel AA fire. First, having learnt that its fuel tanks were prone to being punctured and set on fire, Soviet engineers lined it with polyurethane foam to reduce the danger of fire and explosion. More actively, all Mi-6s operating in Afghanistan were retrofitted with ASO flare-launchers but efforts to install baffles to reduce its infrared signature foundered on the sheer power of its massive Soloviev D-25V turboshaft engines. Their use also changed, with almost all its missions being flown at night from 1986, their running lights off except during take-off and landing, radio traffic kept to a minimum and often a pair of Mi-8MTs or even Mi-24s as escort, depending on the risks of each particular mission. Furthermore, the Soviets introduced a dedicated training programme for Mi-6 pilots being sent to Afghanistan at a mountain training ground near Chirchik and also in a desert facility near Bukhara, based on a similar one already in use for Mi-8 pilots. There, they would spend up to three weeks being drilled in the specific circumstances of Afghanistan, various techniques previous pilots had learnt such as for a rapid, corkscrewing descent into 'hot' landing zones. Even so, they were banned from personnel flights because of the risks until during the withdrawal, when the need to move troops quickly became so pressing that Major General Romanenko, commander of the 40th Army air forces, approved a plan for them to be used for evacuations, but only if they flew at night and each passenger was equipped with a parachute. In a month, four Mi-6s of the 280th OVP had managed to transport some 7,000 soldiers from far-flung bases, typically carrying 50 men at a time, and flying one or two round trips per night.

Mohammad Najibullah reviewing Red Army soldiers marching through Kabul in October 1986. At the time, he was Moscow's great hope to turn the war around, but eventually he would be hanged in that same city in 1996 when the Taliban stormed the UN compound where he had sought shelter. (Daniel Janin/AFP via Getty Images)

Likewise, improvised technical fixes were adopted more widely. Whereas most fixed-wing aircraft were typically rotated in and out of Afghanistan with their crews, the helicopters were generally left in place so as to minimize interruptions in their activity and the effort of transporting them. It was thus pot luck whether a new crew would get a 'zero' – a newly commissioned craft – or something already with hundreds of hours of tough use. A typical Mi-24, for example, would clock up 360–450 flight hours a year in Afghanistan, out of the planned life expectancy before scrappage or total overhaul of 1,000 hours. Flight and ground crews became very experienced with a wide range of field hacks, from starting engines with the batteries from tanks and IFVs to using compressed air meant for other purposes to clear air filters clogged with dust and sand.

## Impact

In that context, it is all the more surprising that, having learnt so many lessons in the hard school of Afghanistan, the Soviet military assiduously and deliberately forgot most of them. The notion in 1989 was that Moscow would never be so foolish as to allow itself to be sucked again into a counter-insurgency war in a mountainous Islamic country and instead it had to pivot back to its core mission of being able to fight a major mechanized war on the plains of Europe. There was a fierce behind-the-scenes debate about this, but ultimately it was felt that while many valuable technical lessons had been learnt and would be retained, the tactical and doctrinal ones would actually detract from this mission. With the partial exception of the VDV paratroopers and *Spetsnaz* special forces, the lessons of Afghanistan were all but purged from the Soviet military's institutional memory.

Of course, the sad irony is that the next war Moscow would wage was in the post-Soviet 1990s, a bid to prevent Chechnya from seceding from the Russian Federation. Again, Russian soldiers would find themselves fighting a counter-insurgency war in a mountainous Islamic country, and so many of the same lessons had painfully to be relearnt.

## After the withdrawal

Nonetheless, this was as nothing to the fate of the DRA's forces. For a while, they proved equal to the difficult task ahead of them. Najibullah proved an able political operator, pitting

The abandoned wrecks of Afghan Air Force Su-7 fighters and Su-17 fighter-bombers at Shindand airbase. (Jonathan Saruk/Getty Images)

tribe against faction, moderate rebel against hard-liner. The DRA forces in their own way also managed to cope – they did not even try to hold all of the country, but just the main cities, even in the face of coordinated *mujahideen* attacks. In 1989, for example, the DRA fought off a 10,000-strong rebel army largely brought together by Pakistan's Inter-Services Intelligence (ISI) agency determined to try to take Jalalabad. This involved not just tough fighting on the ground, but an unprecedentedly high tempo of DRA Air Force sorties, including the use of An-12 transports, modified to drop cluster bombs from sufficiently high altitudes to be out of Stinger range.

However, an attempted coup of elements of the Khalq faction within the PDPA – by now known as the Watan, or National Party – severely weakened Najibullah's position, especially with the defection of Defence Minister Shahnawaz Tanai. The death blow was the collapse of the USSR at the end of 1991, as Boris Yeltsin's new Russian government flatly refused to continue to provide aid to Kabul. Although Najibullah's regime held on briefly, it collapsed in April 1992 and Kabul became the prize fought over by Massoud, Gulbuddin Hekmatyar and former DRA commander Abdul Rashid Dostum. The air force had suffered especially badly from the end of the supply of spare parts and fuel from the USSR, and through the 1990s the number of usable aircraft in Afghanistan dwindled steadily, until by 2000 there were no more than a handful of helicopters still working.

Meanwhile, the *Afgantsy* who had been expected to become the next generation senior commanders reshaping the Soviet army and air forces with the lessons of the war found themselves in a country grinding towards collapse. Some of them became politicians like Gromov and Rutskoi, some became rebels like Dudayev, but none of them would truly have the chance to apply what they had learnt. Instead, Afghanistan became an almost mythical cautionary tale. As one former Su-25 pilot admitted in 1991: 'I served two tours in *Afgan*, I got my major's star there, but already, when I hear people talking about the war, they seem to be talking about a totally different war, one where planes were falling out of the sky every day, and we were carpet-bombing civilians for the hell of it… Who is going to tell the real story of what we "blue-suits" did there?'

# FURTHER READING

Braithwaite, Rodric, *Afgantsy: The Russians in Afghanistan, 1979–89* (Profile, London 2011)

Grau, Lester, *The Bear Went Over the Mountain* (Frank Cass, Abingdon 1998)

Grau, Lester & Michael Gress (eds), *The Soviet-Afghan War. How a superpower fought and lost* (University Press of Kansas, 2002)

Jalali, Ali Ahmad & Lester Grau, *Afghan Guerrilla Warfare. In the Words of a Mujahideen Fighter* (MBI, 2001)

Liakhovsky, Alexander, *Tragediya i Doblest Afgana* (Iskona, Moscow, 1995)

Markovskii, Viktor, *Vyzhzhennoe Nebo Afgana. Boevaya aviatsiya v Afganskoi Voine* (Yauza, Moscow, 2011)

Runov, Valentin, *Afganskaya Voina. Boyevye operatsii* (Eksmo, Moscow 2010)

Urban, Mark, *War in Afghanistan,* 2nd edition (Macmillan, London 1990)

# GLOSSARY

| | |
|---|---|
| 40 OA | *40-ya Obshchevoiskovaya Armiya*: 40th Combined Arms (lit, 'All-Arms') Army |
| AA | *Armeiskaya Aviatsiya*: Army Aviation |
| APC | Armoured Personnel Carrier |
| ATGM | Anti-Tank Guided Missile |
| BAP | *Bombardirovochnny Aviatsionny Polk*: Bomber Aviation Regiment |
| DA | *Dalnaya Aviatsiya*: Long-Range Aviation (ie, Bomber Command) |
| DRA | Democratic Republic of Afghanistan |
| DShB | *Desantno-Shturmovaya Brigada*: Assault Landing Brigade |
| FA | *Frontovaya Aviatsiya*: Frontal Aviation (ie, battlefield air support) |
| GRU | *Glavnoye Razvedyvatelnoye Upravleniye*: Main Intelligence Directorate (of the General Staff), military intelligence |
| HMG | Heavy Machine Gun |
| IAP | *Istrebitelny Aviatsionny Polk*: Fighter Aviation Regiment |
| IBAP | *Istrebitelno-Bombardirovochny Aviatsionny Polk*: Fighter-Bomber Aviation Regiment |
| IED | Improvised Explosive Device |
| IFV | Infantry Fighting Vehicle |
| KGB | *Komitet Gosudarstvennoi Bezopasnosti*: Committee of State Security |
| KhAD | *Khadimat-e-Atalat-e Dawlati*: Afghanistan's State Intelligence Agency |
| MANPADS | Man-Portable Air Defence System (ie, shoulder-fired surface-to-air missile) |
| OAE | *Otdelnaya Aviationnaya Eskadrilya*: Separate Aviation Squadron |
| OBO | *Otdelny Batalon Okrany*: Separate Guard Battalion |
| OKSVA | *Ogranichenny Kontingent Sovetskikh Voisk v Afganistane*: Limited Contingent of Soviet Forces in Afghanistan (sometimes just OKSV) |
| OSAP | *Otdelny Smeshanny Aviatsionny Polk*: Separate Mixed Aviation Regiment |
| OShAE | *Otdelnaya Shturmovaya Aviatsionnaya Eskadrilya*: Separate Attack Aviation Squadron |
| OShAP | *Otdelny Shturmovy Aviatsionny Polk*: Separate Attack Aviation Regiment |
| OSN | *Otryad Spetsialnovo Naznacheniya*: Special Designation Detachment (a *Spetsnaz* unit equivalent to a battalion) |
| OVE | *Otdelnaya Vertolotnaya Aviatsionnaya Eskadrilya*: Separate Helicopter Aviation Squadron |
| OVP | *Otdelny Vertolyotny Polk*: Separate Helicopter Aviation Regiment |
| PDPA | People's Democratic Party of Afghanistan |
| RUD | *Razvedyvatelno-Udarnye Dyeystviya*: Reconnaissance-Strike Action |
| SAM | Surface-to-Air Missile |
| *Sarandoy* | 'Defenders', the PDPA's paramilitary gendarmerie, part of the Interior Ministry |
| *Spetsnaz* | *Spetsialnovo Naznacheniya*: Special Purpose, ie, special forces (literally, Special Designation) |
| TBAP | *Tyazholy Bombardirovochny Aviatsionny Polk*: Heavy Bomber Aviation Regiment |
| TurkVO | *Turkestansky Voyenny Okrug*: Turkestan Military District |
| VDV | *Vozdushno-Desantnye Voiska*: Air Assault Troops (ie, paratroopers) |
| VTA | *Voyennaya Transportnaya Aviatsiya*: Military Transport Aviation |
| VTAP | *Voyenny Transportny Aviatsionny Polk*: Military Transport Aviation Regiment |

# INDEX